M000012932

HARBORS

Harbors

© 2016 Donald Quist

Second printing, 2018

Published by Awst Press
P.O. Box 49163
Austin, TX 78765

awst-press.com
awst@awst-press.org

Printed in the United States of America
Distributed by Small Press Distribution

ISBN: 978-0-9971938-1-7
Library of Congress Control Number: 2016942994

Cover illustration by Maggie Chiang
Editing by Tatiana Ryckman
Copyediting by Emily Roberts
Book design by LK James

In memory of
Thelma R. Hines & Paulina Hans-Quist

There lies the port; the vessel puffs her sail:
There gloom the dark, broad seas. My mariners,
Souls that have toil'd, and wrought, and thought with me—
That ever with a frolic welcome took
The thunder and the sunshine, and opposed
Free hearts, free foreheads—you and I are old;
Old age hath yet his honour and his toil;
Death closes all: but something ere the end,
Some work of noble note, may yet be done,

—Alfred Lord Tennyson, "Ulysses"

~ ~ ~ ~

and may you in your innocence
sail through this to that

—Lucille Clifton, "blessing the boats"

CONTENTS

HARBORS

Genevieve, ~~DONALD QUIST~~ 3/6/20

Thank you so much for your
Interest in my work. I look
forward to seeing more
of your writing in the
world.

THROUGH THIS / TO STRIVE, TO SEEK :
LOG I

RAYS

THE WOLVERINE

I have a scar, a scaly callus on my right pinky knuckle from when I cut my hand on Ray Nelson's teeth. The day I ripped my fist on his incisors, Ray had snatched my Wolverine action figure. I spent nearly half an hour chasing him along the tulip tree line of the forest bordering our elementary school playground. Whenever I stopped to catch my breath he made sure to keep a few meters distance between us. During these respites, I scanned to see if any of the other kids might be laughing at me. On the kickball field, at the basketball courts, and atop the rusting metal jungle gyms, my fourth grade classmates celebrated the end of winter in Maryland and the return of outdoor recess. I lamented the return of outdoor recess. The grown-ups could not monitor the expanse of the schoolyard all at once. This left me susceptible to getting pushed into mud puddles or getting grass clippings and wood chips shoved into my underwear, or having something I cherished taken by little red-headed dweebs like Ray Nelson.

When I tired of the chase, I sprinted over to Ms. Orsega who was posted by the side entrance doors of the school. I nearly cried as I whined to her about the egregiousness of the theft. I tried to explain to Ms. Orsega that everyone, and by everyone I meant every boy in the fourth grade, coveted Wolverine. By demonstrating his posable limbs and retractable claws during

Show and Tell, I believed I could bond with my tormentors and possibly befriend them. She listened, arms folded, her silver whistle resting between her lips. When I finished she blew a strident blast.

Ray stood watching and waiting several feet away. He began inching further towards the soccer field. Ms. Orsega beckoned him with a finger, and Ray shuffled closer with his eyes on the ground.

"Give it back," she said.

"Give what back?" he said, pulling Wolverine behind him.

"The doll," she said.

Ray and I corrected her in unison: "It's not a doll!"

"Whatever. Give it back."

And Ray did. I extended my left hand and Wolverine was returned to me.

"Okay?" she asked me.

A cluster of kids who rode the bus to school with Ray and me gathered around. They followed the scream of Ms. Orsega's whistle with the expectation of seeing one of us castigated.

I thought of Wolverine, not the one in my possession, the real one in the comics and cartoons. He didn't need an intercessor. Wolverine sliced bullies with adamantium claws.

What would Wolverine have done?

I imagined weapons like knives sprouting from my fist as I struck Ray's face. I reached back to hit him again, but Ms. Orsega hooked the collar of my shirt. I almost punched at her to get loose before I noticed the blood, my knuckle, Ray's mouth, and half of a single tooth cupped in the palms of his red, quivering hands.

GREEN BUS KIDS

At Galway Elementary School, you could always spot the kids who rode the green bus. They seemed to fight for no reason. When belongings vanished from classroom cubbies, they were often found in the holey pockets of the kids who rode the green bus. You could identify those kids by their free lunches and their hand-me-downs. Every Halloween they wore the cheap drugstore costumes comprised of a vinyl smock and a flimsy plastic mask with a thin elastic band. They didn't bring candy for Valentine's Day and they never passed out birthday party invitations. They lived in the Windsor Towers apartment complex, those beige stucco cinder block towers behind the shopping plaza on Columbia Pike. On hot days the sour stench of rotten grocery store produce and wasted Chuck E. Cheese's pizza would waft up from the dumpsters in back of the Safeway. Sometimes the rot stuck to those kids who rode the green bus. They'd carry the stink to school. The kids with scars they chose not to explain, kids like Ray and me.

The school assigned each bus an arbitrary color and taped a laminated piece of construction paper on the right window above the first row of passenger seats. The pigment of the paper in the window helped students remember which vehicle took them home. The green bus that Ray and I rode looked like all the others, big and yellow, but our drivers had a higher turnover rate.

Of all the drivers, I only remember one: a large woman shaped like a deflating balloon. Air escaped from her mouth in wheezy sighs and exasperated shouts. One day after school, the balloon lady parked the bus on Castle Boulevard, half a mile from Windsor Towers. She refused to take us any further if we didn't quiet down and start showing her some respect. Inevitably, she pulled the keys from the ignition, yanked the lever that caused the heavy doors of the bus to swing open, and walked off.

We waited silently, hoping our new stillness would cause her to reappear. Once we understood that she would not return, some children went in search of a pay phone. The rest of us, myself and Ray included, walked home.

Sometimes I'd think of that bus driver and wonder what became of her. Maybe the administrators sympathized with her wanting to abandon us. Maybe she asked for a transfer to the orange bus with the children from the big detached houses in Tanglewood. Maybe the balloon lady would enjoy chauffeuring the kids who brought their lunches to school, kids who didn't feel compelled to punch or steal.

SCARS

Because of his freckles, orange hair, and upturned nose, Ray stood out among the few white children living in Windsor Towers. When the other green bus kids grew bored criticizing my weight, glasses, and bookishness, they battered Ray.

Children can swing sharp, cleaving insults; like tiny butchers, they chop down hard for deep cuts. A rumor about Ray's single mother not having a job and sleeping with men for rent money circulated among the kids in Windsor Towers. Even some of the kids from the neighboring low-rise apartments in Windsor Courts teased Ray about his prostituting mother.

But Ray's mother did have a real job. I discovered this the day I slugged him.

Ray and I sat next to each other in the lobby of Galway's administrative offices while the principal phoned our parents. Still whimpering, Ray held an ice gel pack wrapped in a washcloth pressed to the left side of his face. It had taken the nurse several minutes to calm Ray down and ease his hyperventilating. She managed to get him to stand in front of a sink, rinse his mouth with warm water, and spit out any remaining shards of tooth. When Ray finished, she gave him some cotton balls and instructed him to squish them into his mouth. He had soaked his shirt with pink saliva, so the nurse stripped it off and gave him a dry but dingy tee from the lost and found. The nurse then turned to me. She told me to wash my hand in the same sink speckled by Ray's DNA. His blood and mine swirled together at the bottom of the stainless steel basin. The nurse dumped peroxide on the wound, and the bubbling liquid felt like a colony of invisible ants crawling over my open knuckle. She dried the deep cut carefully with rough brown paper towels and then dressed it with the biggest adhesive bandage she had. Not nearly strong enough to pull the sides of my laceration together, the grape-scented sticky strip lay like a purple bridge across the fissure of flesh. I had stained the front bottom of my shirt wrapping and cradling my bleeding fist, but nothing in the lost and found would fit me.

The bandage began falling off by the time the nurse brought Ray and me to the principal's office. I folded my fist back into my crimson-spotted shirt. Sweating from the pain, Ray's hair matted against his forehead. We reeked of rust.

When the principal emerged from behind his office door, even though his eyes focused on Ray and me, he spoke only to the receptionist. The receptionist also watched us from across her desk while the principal explained that he had informed my mother of what had happened and that she would soon come to pick me up from school. Ray's mother would not be able to collect Ray because she couldn't find anyone to cover her shift at work.

I glanced at Ray. His mother had a proper job with mandatory hours. I wondered why he never bothered to correct classmates when they slapped the back of his head and called his momma a broke ho.

The principal added that Ray and I rode the green bus. This detail seemed to mean something to the principal and his receptionist, and they nodded in a shared understanding.

"No one else can pick you up from school?" the receptionist asked Ray.

Ray shook his head slowly and then winced from the pain in his mouth.

The principal returned to his office. The receptionist stood up and walked around her desk. When she got close enough, she placed a hand on Ray's shoulder. She told me to stay seated and that she'd return after escorting Ray to his classroom. I watched Ray rise slowly to his feet, and he and the receptionist left the lobby.

On the green bus, Charles Smiley served as a frequent instigator of taunts and physical assaults. He dubbed me Fat Urkel after tripping me into a hedge of conifers in front of my father's apartment building. As I fell Charles exclaimed, "Did I do that?" The moniker became so popular it traveled back to school and for a few months many of the students, even some of the preppy orange bus kids, forgot my real name.

Ray remembered my real name. Even though Ray laughed along with the crowd of green bus kids watching me struggle to climb out from under the coarse branches and prickly leaves of the hedge, Ray stayed after all the others dispersed. He asked if the fall hurt, and I told him to fuck off. I suspected Ray's question was a simple act of compassion, that maybe he saw in me a fellow victim, someone with whom he might identify. But I didn't dare display any interest in him beyond casual acquaintance for fear that an apparent friendship between the whore's son and Fat Urkel might warrant further ridicule from our peers.

Maybe an unspoken alliance had led me to summon Ray to the edge of the school playground to show him the Wolverine I had so safely guarded in my backpack, because I knew he'd appreciate the significance of that doll. Perhaps Ray tried to take the Wolverine because he recognized that six inches of molded posable plastic had the potential to improve the quality of his life, and when faced with an absurdity like this a person might feel desperate enough to take what they do not own.

But I didn't think of Ray while the school nurse walked him to his classroom. I sat alone in the office lobby, bleeding into my shirt, and dwelling on how the principal had confiscated my Wolverine. I did not think about how the other green bus kids might treat Ray now that he'd had a tooth knocked out of his head by Fat Urkel.

RAYS

My mother didn't yell on the forty-minute car ride to her townhouse. She chided me for a short while and then moved into a grumbly rant about the quality of the kids in Windsor Towers. She did this whenever she collected me from my dad's place and noticed my torn clothes and bruises. My mother often blamed herself. She'd say she never should have enrolled me in a school so far away from her home. She'd swear to remove me, if I really wanted, but we both knew that the proximity of Galway Elementary to her job and my father's apartment meant not having to pay for childcare. Sometimes she'd ask, "Who hurt you?" I never gave her a name. I refused to implicate Charles Smiley or the others. I knew it would lead to retaliation.

However, on that day my mother picked me up from school, the principal had finally given her a name, Ray Nelson. In the car, mom made heated assumptions about the type of person she believed Ray to be. She told me that Ray and all the other children in Windsor Towers couldn't conceal their jealousy. They didn't like me because they knew I didn't belong with them. I resembled the kids that lived in Tanglewood, the orange bus kids. I leaned my head against the passenger side door and watched the solid yellow line on the narrow county highway rise and fall with the hills. My mother's words began to melt into each other, blurring like the blooming trees and glades rushing past my window.

That night, my mom phoned my father to tell him what had happened. He asked to speak to me. After repeating a lot of what my mother had said, my dad asked if I had won the fight. I didn't know how to answer initially. Maybe in that moment I thought of the Wolverine again, not the action figure but the intellectual property named after an animal known for its ferocity and solitude. I said yes. The other side of the telephone went quiet and in that silent pause I heard my father's relief. He said that the other kids probably wouldn't tease me anymore because now they knew I would stand up for myself.

I never spoke to Ray Nelson after the day I hit him. He and his mother eventually moved out of Windsor Towers. I last saw Ray during my first winter in middle school. That day some boys planned to attack me in retaliation for me punching Charles Smiley in the stomach. Four pairs of salt-stained Timberland boots stomped down on my arched back. My knees pressed firm against the icy pathway leading into my father's apartment building. With each kick and blow my bare knuckles ground into the concrete. Ray walked past while those boys cut me down. A heavy boot thwacked against the rear of my skull and I felt a stinging in my teeth. Ray's eyes met mine briefly and then he returned his attention to the cracked sidewalk under his feet. He went on, one leg following the other.

CLOSING PROCEDURES
AT SPENCER GIFTS

1.A

Spend the last hour of your last day at Spencer's hiding from potential customers. In the narrow walkway between a row of shelves and the back wall of the retail space, sit cross-legged on the black rubber floor tiles. Above the dark aisle, long ultraviolet bulbs replace the normal fluorescent ceiling lights. On the wall where three smaller UV lamps hang over a horizontal line of psychedelic posters, press your spine against a glowing neon portrait of Jim Morrison.

1.B

On the other side of the dimly lit aisle, sex toys, flavored condoms, and penis-shaped candies pack the shelves. Pull a box of edible panties from its place. Read and reread the ingredients, because you are fascinated by their similarity to Fruit Roll-Ups. Consider setting up a display for the new sale items, stocking shelves, counting inventory—the things you should be doing.

1.C

As a sales associate, you should be at the front entrance greeting passersby and luring them inside with details about discounted products. Your job description involves creating a vision for consumers, showing them how Spencer's can enliven any social situation or gathering. Instead, you are admiring the way the stains on your shirt explode in the black light.

How many months have passed since you washed the blood-colored polo? At sixteen, doing laundry is less of a priority. Your work clothes always reek of the store: a combination of incense sticks and burning plastic.

1.D

Listen to *The Slim Shady LP* play on the overhead speakers as the other sales associate, Nathan, zips through the aisles on a compact folding scooter he removed from its packaging. Laughing wickedly, he raps along with Eminem, "I just drank a fifth of vodka, dare me to drive?"

1.E

If anyone ever asks you why Nathan replaced the music compilations approved by Spencer's corporate office with compact discs from his car, do not mention how the idea came to him while carrying stolen merchandise out to the trunk of his sedan. Forget the fog machine and the two strobe lights Nathan snatched from the store's front window display.

Nathan does not expect you to report the items he has stolen. He started two weeks ago and you have never been scheduled to work together. You don't know anything about him except that he attends a rival high school. You don't even know his last name. His trust in you is undeserved. But you both share mutual acquaintances and a familiar space. You and Nathan wear the same uniform, and this makes you comrades.

1.F

Understand that Nathan won't be caught. There are no closed circuit cameras, no theft detection system, and no security gates at the entrance. Cory, the former manager, told you that your store plays an important role in loss prevention. "People steal," she said. "There's no point in pretending they won't. Some can't help themselves. It's better they steal an overpriced tchotchke from us than something really valuable from another part of the mall." Cory understood things like capitalism and human nature and how Spencer's at Lakeforest Mall in Gaithersburg, Maryland relates to everything.

Most of the inventory is easy to conceal and can slide comfortably into a coat pocket or down a pant leg. The crowded shelving creates tight corners and blocks lines of sight from the cash registers. The store is a darkened mini-maze with over a dozen places to hide.

Cory instructed you never to confront shoplifters. She said it wasn't worth risking an altercation. She never said what you should do if you saw a coworker stealing.

1.G

Nathan skids up to you and hops down from the scooter. The blond freckles that spread across his arms and face vanish under the UV lights. He turns violet as he steps closer.

When Nathan asks you if you plan to take anything, shrug and tell him you haven't decided yet.

Nathan rolls his eyes. He reminds you that none of it matters anyway. In the days that follow, any large items missing from the store can be charged to Cory, who has disappeared. It is likely both you and Nathan will be looking for new jobs in a week.

2.A

Think back, and remember the morning.

2.B

Remember the district manager's face from earlier, puffy and pink like she had just risen from bed. Remember how she glanced over you and Nathan without introducing herself or asking for your names. When the district manager squatted to unlock the rolling steel gate guarding the front of the store, the seams of her black spandex pants threatened to burst. She muttered to herself as she tried half a dozen keys hanging from her lanyard. And you thought about how each one of those keys represented another Spencer's. Different locations at malls just like this one, with sales associates just like you. You tried to imagine the responsibility that comes with all those keys and your guts churned.

2.C

Once inside, the district manager went to the cash registers. You and Nathan prepared for customers, which involves refolding novelty T-shirts, flipping on a dozen power strips, and sweeping. While you worked, Nathan quietly speculated on Cory's whereabouts and why she hadn't come to open the store. One of Nathan's imagined scenarios involved Cory embezzling money to pay for a sex change operation. The other involved Cory committing suicide. In either event, Nathan believed Cory had taken money and he made predictions on whether the district manager would discover the bank bag missing from the store's safe.

2.D

While you swept, you saw a lone mop string on the floor, a remnant of the previous night's cleaning. You bent down to pick it up. The long, thin, grey rope smelled like saltwater and bleach. It resembled something that had once lived, the tentacle of some strange cephalopod. The tight cotton coils of the mop string looked like muscle, and a thread of reddish hair traced over them like a vein.

That hair could have belonged to Cory. She might have stood right where you were standing. She was there and then she wasn't.

2.E

Staring at the mop string, you remembered how in the weeks leading up to Cory's absence, she had often shown up late. Sometimes she smelled sour and unwashed with cigarette smoke and stale beer trapped in the thick tangles of her auburn hair. Recently, she had even forgotten to make a work schedule for the employees.

A few days earlier, you had walked into the stock room and found Cory crying. She sat on a pallet of South Park–themed coin banks, muffling her heavy sobs with a fist. When Cory finally acknowledged you, she shook her head slowly and said, "We're lucky you know? I've got benefits here. People can't find work. There are people starving." Her voice sounded like someone else. She waved a hand over all the merchandise around you and said, "We're doing a hell of a lot better than the people forced to make this crap."

Then she didn't seem to care that you were in the room anymore. Her body shuddered as she tried to swallow the groans rising from her belly. You stood frozen near the door, too scared to speak or move. You watched Cory bite down on her fingers while rivulets of tears smeared her eyeshadow.

2.F

You hadn't mentioned that moment to anyone. Tossing the mop string into Nathan's dustpan, you wish you could understand the cause of Cory's apparent sadness. You wish you could pin it between your fingers like a single dirty cord.

2.G

The district manager called to you and Nathan from the register, "Where's the safe?" Before Nathan could answer, the district manager pointed at you. She told Nathan to stand at the front and handle any customers. You led her to the back of the store and through the swinging door with the Employees Only sign.

2.H

The district manager pulled out Cory's chair and sat down. The store safe, as deep and as wide as a single file cabinet, sat under Cory's desk. Its black paint had several scratches from having been dragged and rolled.

The district manager spun the dial of the combination lock.

"Are you the one who called me collect this morning from a payphone?" she asked.

You said yes.

She asked for your name and you told her, tucking the nametag hanging from your neck into your shirt. A month earlier when Cory had begun to stop caring, you had used a pricing gun to decorate your store ID with $69.69 stickers. You feared the district manager would not find it as funny as you did.

The door of the safe popped open and the district manager paused to ask you how you got her number. You explained to her how you dialed 411, called the Spencer's at White Flint Mall, and they gave you the contact information.

"Pretty smart," the district manager said.

The district manager rummaged through the contents of the safe and removed the bank deposit bag. You sighed, relieved at the sight of the vinyl envelope fat with the previous day's cash. The district manager tucked the bank bag under her arm. She slammed the safe door and gave the dial a final twist.

"I spoke to Cory," the district manager said. "I called her after you called me. She didn't answer at first. I kept calling until finally she picks up and says, 'I'll mail you the keys,' and then click, dial tone."

You nodded to show you understood even though you didn't.

The district manager asked you if there was anything she needed to know about Cory. You contemplated telling her about Cory crying in the stock room but decided against it. Instead you told the district manager that Cory had seemed unhappy.

A thin smile spread over the district manager's mouth.

"Unhappy." She chuckled and the fat under her chin jiggled. "It's a job."

The district manager stood, grabbed a blank receipt and a pen from the desk, wrote her number on the paper, and passed it to you. She said there would be restructuring. She told you she would need someone who could tell her who would be worth keeping around. The district manager promised you that there would be a place for you at Spencer's if you wanted it.

2.1

Before leaving, the district manager told you she would return in the evening. She contacted a manager at another location to relieve you and Nathan at the end of your scheduled work shift. You and Nathan are in charge until then. The district manager assured you that she had checked the balance of both registers. If the registers have money missing at the close of the day, she will hold you responsible.

However, the store doesn't have many customers on Saturday mornings, and with fewer transactions there exists less opportunity to steal money from the drawers of the register. In the hours since the district manager left, you have made only one sale to a girl who attends Nathan's high school. She bought a Playboy belly button ring and a steel hip flask. As you handed her change, a group of three middle school boys came into the store. They separated at the front entrance, each taking their own aisle. The boys congregated again around the adult greeting cards. Their hands never seemed to rest, picking up a card, putting it down, picking up another one and putting it down. A few times you noticed their eyes dart from Nathan to you and back to Nathan. Whenever you caught their gaze, they'd turn their heads away. There were snickers and whispers. The hands disappeared into jeans and jackets, and the boys hustled out of the store in silence.

3.A

Return the box of edible panties to its shelf. Retrieve the receipt paper with the district manager's number from your pocket. Pass the district manager's number to Nathan.

Nathan asks you, "What is this?"

Ignore the question. Ask him why neither of you tried to stop the three boys this morning.

He reminds you that Cory told the staff not to bust shoplifters.

You remind him that Cory no longer serves as the manager of Spencer Gifts at Lakeforest Mall.

Nathan says, "Fine."

Then Nathan says, "I don't see the point in calling mall security just because some kids took a birthday card with a naked lady on it. It doesn't seem worth it."

You ask him why.

"Nobody is going to miss it, just like nobody's going to miss the stuff I took out of here. And why should we care anyway? What are we even doing here, man? The district manager is probably going to fire us all. She's going to bring in new people and a manager she can trust."

Restructuring.

Nathan returns his focus to the receipt paper in his hands. "What is this?"

You tell him about the district manager giving you her number.

Nathan falls quiet. He raises an eyebrow and asks if you plan to rat on him.
You say no.
Nathan nods.

3.B

Get up from the floor and brush off your pants. Nathan offers to bring back the items he has taken. He says he doesn't want to get you into trouble. You tell him not to worry about it. It doesn't matter.

3.C

Reach for the handlebars and pull the scooter away from Nathan. Place one foot on the deck and kick off with the other. Coast past inflatable dolls, past beer funnels, past shot glasses, past drinking board games.

Think about Cory. Had she known yesterday she'd quit or did she surprise herself? You have questions you may never be able to ask her. Realize you barely know anything about the person who has signed your paychecks. You have gathered that Cory has no children. She has mentioned a boyfriend. You know that she has worked at Spencer's for nearly a decade. Cory appeared to be in her thirties, maybe a little older than the district manager.

Try to imagine yourself as Cory, as a store manager. Then try to envision being the district manager. Try to imagine heavy sets of keys hanging on a rope around your neck or on a carabineer clipped to your sagging belt.

Make a sharp turn and push past lava lamps, past collectible action figures and detailed models, past plush toys, past gag gifts and whoopee cushions and rubber chickens.

Words like Globalization and Consumerism tie you to the other side of the world and the people who slave to make the things you call novelties. Somewhere else people starve. Someone else steals because they have too little. It is unfortunate, but you are not them.

3.E

Push for the exit, past the registers and the body jewelry display case, past Zippos, past funny hats and hoodies, past shirts with Bob Marley and pot leaves. Push past chain wallets and iron-on patches, past messenger bags and band posters. Kick your leg out and push the scooter past the entrance of the store, past the f.y.e., past the Cinnabon, past the payphone where you called the district manager.

And then, push harder.

3.F

Return the scooter to Spencer's.

Never come back.

TANGLEWOOD

The last line hangs from your bottom lip, dry and chapped. You set your manuscript down on the stool, pick up a bottle of water, and try to swallow the remainder of your trepidation. The teacher, Ms. Inga Puffer—whom you admire for being both gracious and brave enough to have invited you to Tanglewood Middle School to read some of your fiction to her students—asks the class for questions.

A dozen tiny hands point to the ceiling and fear creeps over you. You count slowly to five. Standing to your full height, your chest swells with the fake confidence of a man with nothing to lose but his pride. You are naked and bleeding in a tank of piranha.

There is a boy with hair pulled tightly into the most elegant cornrows you have ever seen. He's smaller than the others and sits on his knees, hyper-extending his arm above the crowd. The other kids collectively sigh as you acknowledge him. He reminds them they are not near as old as they pretend.

"Were you nervous just then, reading that? You sounded nervous sometimes."

His question confirms your suspicion that twelve-year-olds are every bit as perceptive as they've always been.

"Yeah, I was a little nervous. I don't really get a chance to read my stuff all that much and I worry if it's good or not."

The classroom roars, children speaking out of turn:

"I'd buy that book!"

"Me, too."

"That's something I would read."

"I like to read and I'd read that."

"It's good."

"Yeah, it's great."

"It's awesome."

A cacophony of pubescent voices answers the question always tugging at your heart.

Yes, your work could matter to someone.

You can't stop beaming. It only took thirteen years but you are finally popular with middle school kids. You think back to when you were their age. In the seventh grade you were a black, sexually ambiguous Francophile communist vampire, stalking the halls in a heavy winter trench coat, dark colored everything, and a black beret. Eccentric isn't the word for it. It is a moment in your life of which you are eternally grateful there are no pictures; candid, glossy, four-by-six memories that would squash any chances of a career in politics. Sitting in the back of the class, bubble gum cigarette dangling from the corner of your mouth, arms folded, nose buried in a science fiction novel or your tattered paperback copy of *The Communist Manifesto*, you deflected any teachers' attempts at bettering you with snarky quips and flimsy logic. "No. Of course I didn't do my homework. I'm a communist, duh!" You spent a hundred nights pecking at the keys of a typewriter, producing a thirty–four–page novella riddled with major spelling errors and devoid of structure or premise. Everything about you was pretentious and hypocritical, and it was reflected in your work. But you couldn't see it then. You carried your manuscript with you at all times in case the world decided to notice your genius and make you dirty rich. Your actions proved you were still enamored of the capitalist dogma you preached against. Your actions warranted the near daily ass-kickings from your peers.

You wonder if these students are as misguided as you were.

You manage to squeak, "Thanks."

The kids have settled down with a little coaxing from Ms. Puffer. Their hands have risen again for questions. You see a girl in your peripheral vision.

She is rail thin but carries the confidence of a three-hundred-pound professional athlete. She was one of the ones who stayed quiet while the others drowned you in praise.

You point to her and say, "Um, okay. You."

She pulls her hand down slowly. "I'm Tiesha Blakley."

"Yes?"

"Why did you want to be a writer?"

Why?

In the tenth grade you weren't old enough to smoke but you did it anyway. Though you had abandoned communism and surrendered your beret, your predilection for Hawaiian shirts still made you undateable. You weren't an outcast anymore but your circle of friends didn't share your love of language. You still harbored aspirations of piecing together something worthy of acclaim. You began to keep your writing secret, fearing criticism like that you received in the eighth grade when Charles Smiley got ahold of your backpack and read some of your poetry aloud on the bus to school. You tried to attack him, but you had yet to learn how to fight and the only thing your brief experience with karate had taught you was how to look really cool breaking stuff. You were slow and clumsy like long division, and Charles overpowered you like Algebra II. When your father picked you up from the principal's office, he asked if you had won. You told him no. He didn't bother hiding his disappointment. He asked you why. "Because I'm a writer, Dad!" He asked you if you were gay. You told him no. But he didn't seem entirely convinced.

He'd ask you again in the twelfth grade when you told him you were going to college to learn how to become an author. Your freshman academic writing course proved that prose didn't come to you as naturally as you had hoped. Writing soon became something to work towards. It was about realizing what your professors called "potential." You had to fight for it; you had to push yourself and show the world that you were worthy of your talents. You found discipline in the text. You wrote for a couple of newspapers, published some short stories, but it never seemed like enough. One night, when the fear of remaining obscure kept you from sleep, you searched old writing for inspiration. You found it in a pile of childhood journals. The writing was awful, histrionic, and self-important, but there were ideas worth exploring. The desire to do better propelled you.

"I write because I am compelled."

Tiesha Blakley and the kids wear their confusion on their faces.

"Redo. I'm just not that good at anything else. I suck at math."

They laugh. They're still yours. You answer more questions about your life and art. Whenever the inquiries get too personal, Ms. Puffer clears her throat and the students ask another. For the most part it's the same question: "Are you happy?"

You find new and creative ways to say yes. You want to tell them the complicated truth—you've found the hardest way to make an easy living. But they wouldn't appreciate the cleverness of your answer. They don't care about your vocabulary. They just like the way your words sound. They like you because you're something new.

A student asks how long you've been writing.

"I guess you could say I've been writing stories since I was ten, but it wasn't until three years ago that I got serious about making work worth printing."

Their mouths hang open, stunned by your commitment.

To them your failures don't matter. They don't care how many of your query letters have gone unanswered, or how few conference panels you've participated in, or the number of residency workshops you've attended. To them, you are what you say you are. Your name, written in dry-erase marker on the giant whiteboard behind you, is no different than those on the spines of books in the school media center.

As Ms. Puffer thanks you for coming, you step outside of yourself for a moment. You try seeing yourself the way the kids do. And when the teacher asks the class if they have any more questions for a "real" author, it's like you've stopped playing pretend. It is the very first time someone has referred to you as a writer and you didn't feel like a fake.

There are no more questions.

TILL NEXT TIME,
TAKE CARE OF YOURSELVES
AND EACH OTHER

I peer down into the casket at her bloated, dry remains. Draped in snowy lace and rested over satin pillows, she looks unlike herself. I regret taking this final glimpse into the coffin before the procession. I would rather remember Thelma the way I most often did in my youth: the Old Lady haloed by cigarette smoke and leaning forward on the edge of a tattered loveseat, watching *The Jerry Springer Show*, her favorite.

She would nod occasionally in acknowledgment of something a guest on the show would say. She'd shake her head like a disapproving parent when fist fights started on stage or someone threw a piece of furniture. Thelma saw the set grow wider and the chairs become lighter as Richard Dominick and the show-runners tried to accommodate the brawls. Eventually, Steve Wilkos could not subdue the fervent guests by himself and the show needed to expand security. Thelma approved of these changes, for safety.

"A few weeks ago, my history teacher said this show is like the gladiator arena in Rome. She said it pacifies the masses and distracts us from our crumbling empire."

"What? Boy, quiet. Jerry's about to give his Final Thought."

"My teacher says Jerry is exploiting these people and this show is bad for society."

Thelma glared down at me sitting cross-legged on the floor by her feet.

She belched a grey cloud of nicotine and said, "Springer is true life."

During his closing statements on episode 51 in season 16, "Update: I Still Love You!," Jerry says, "TV doesn't make truth, nor can it change it."

The show would become more surreal in later seasons in an attempt to raise controversy and television ratings. Some of the revamps included an actor playing a drunken priest to officiate weddings, gelatin wresting, mud wrestling, champagne bubble baths, fight bells and ring card girls, a steel catwalk above the stage leading to a fireman's pole which Jerry and exotic dancers could use as an entrance, and green plastic Mardi Gras–inspired necklaces called "Jerry Beads" that encouraged guests and audience members to flash body parts.

But despite these embellishments, the men and women who came on the show looked and sounded, as the Old Lady suggested, very real. They didn't possess physical features like those other daytime drama stars with clear skin and chiseled frames. The guests on *Springer* seemed familiar and common. Their stories resembled those I'd overhear at my granduncle's house in Hartsville, South Carolina.

I spent most vacations from school sitting in my granduncle's den, pretending to read R.L. Stine or Camus while listening to people pour out their tales of woe to the Old Lady. I can only remember a few of her frequent visitors. Larry struggled with alcoholism and every week he'd arrive to confess his recent missteps and falls from grace. Beulah fretted over her lesbian daughter who had conflicts with lovers all over town. Carrie couldn't stay faithful to her hen-pecked husband. Boo came by as regularly as she could—her addiction to crack cocaine caused her to vanish for months while she served jail time for petty thefts and prostitution.

Day after day, Mondays through Fridays, they came to sit and talk with Thelma in the kitchen or on the front porch. The Old Lady would offer them a short cup of cheap vodka and she would listen, nodding occasionally in acknowledgment, breaking her silence only to ask a sporadic question for clarification. Once the person finished speaking and drained the last drop of spirits from their clear plastic cup, Thelma would posit a final thought for them to consider as they went on their way, and sometimes I'd notice her visitors appeared a little less sad or angry or scared than they had looked before.

~ ~ ~ ~

Few of Thelma's guests have come to help carry her casket to the hearse. Days before the funeral, Larry came to my mother's home weeping incoherently. I fixed him a drink, like the Old Lady would do. I patted him on the back and gave him some cash for a forty-ounce bottle of malt liquor. I watched him stumble down the street, knowing that once I lost sight of him sinking into the horizon he'd never resurface.

Perhaps Thelma's cohorts feel too grief-stricken to come to her memorial service, or maybe they don't feel comfortable in churches. Instead, the warm bodies shuffling from the pews belong to members of the congregation, somber church folks obligated to my granduncle—a valued member of their flock.

My granduncle sings with the men's choir the fourth Sunday of every month. He served on the church treasury committee and with the United Methodist Men's organization for decades. He joins Bible study on Wednesdays and adult Bible school on Sundays before the II a.m. service. He uses his carpentry experience to repair things around the facility.

In contrast, his sister Thelma had never stepped inside this church, or any other, my entire life. But she did have faith. Whenever I stayed at my granduncle's house, the Old Lady made sure to get me ready for church on Sundays. On the occasions I didn't want to go, she'd threaten to withhold dinner or television.

"But you never go. Why do I always have to go?"

"You should give your uncle company. Help me keep an eye on him; make sure he stays out of trouble."

"Those aren't real reasons! Why don't you ever go?"

"God and I have an agreement."

I'd pout and leave with my granduncle, and the Old Lady would turn on a televangelist. She'd dial the volume all the way up while she cooked and cleaned, so the waves of shouts of praise flooded the entire house, immersing her in worship. The next day would replace the cries for Jesus with cheers for "JERRY! JERRY! JERRY!"

At church, people often spoke to me about Thelma.

"I saw your grandmamma fighting with a cashier at the Piggly Wiggly."

"I heard your grandma threatened to shoot somebody at Wash Tub Laundry the other day."

"Your grandmother gave a city councilman the bird when he tried to cut her in line at the bank."

Sometimes, I overheard members of the congregation express sympathy for my granduncle. They'd employ the same adjectives critics use to describe *The Jerry Springer Show*. They called Thelma crass and rude, and pitied my charitable granduncle for allowing her to live with him. They said she'd obviously never be welcomed by anyone else.

Many of the Old Lady's reviewers have come today to offer their condolences. They approach me after the pastor's sermon to offer a warm embrace and to whisper thoughts of encouragement into my ear. I recall many of the same voices years earlier condemning the woman I mourn.

As they line up to hug my granduncle, I can see he grieves too. He usually smiles broadly, but today his face—creased and furrowed with concern—has adopted Thelma's resting scowl. The differences between the siblings have always outnumbered their similarities. My granduncle didn't have much interest in the things Thelma relished. He didn't smoke and rarely drank. He didn't watch daytime television. Although a disabled veteran, he tried to stay active and didn't enjoy staying home during the day like Thelma. Most often, I could find him doing something at church or exercising at the YMCA.

On Tuesdays my granduncle participated in Meals on Wheels, delivering food prepared by the kitchen staff at the local hospital to elderly shut-ins. He often brought me along and let me carry the plates from the car to the houses. I'd knock loudly at each home and wait for several seconds. Usually, the door would creak open. The stale air from inside—reeking of sour flesh, urine, peppermint, and halitosis—would reach out with a pair of shaking paper hands to cradle the foam container.

I'd recollect these images and scents years later while walking into Thelma's room in the intensive care unit at Carolina Pines where she died.

A few times, the door didn't open and I returned to my granduncle's car sulking over the probability that the intended recipient of the meal now only existed in memory. My granduncle and I didn't dare to consume the food left behind. I held these plates in my lap until we reached his house. Thelma would eat the meal or give it to one of her visitors.

~ ~ ~ ~

One day, my granduncle and I returned to the house with a remaining Meals on Wheels plate to discover Thelma standing above a body sprawled onto the living room floor. I quickly set the lunch down and we rushed over to the Old Lady's side. At our feet, Carrie laid facedown, muttering into a pool of her own chunky, beige vomit.

My granduncle shook his head and frowned at Thelma. The Old Lady and I watched him leave. We heard the door to the rear patio slam behind him. Thelma lit a cigarette and took a seat on the plastic covered sofa.

"She had a little too much to drink," Thelma explained. "I want you to clean this up and drive Carrie home in my El Camino."

"No."

"Just do it, boy. I can't be bending down there and she's too heavy for me to get off the ground."

"I only have a learner's permit."

"It's just across the lake. It's a straight shot up Fifth Street, and you'll have an adult in the car with you. Now, help me take care of this."

Thelma stood and walked to the bathroom to fetch cleaning items, leaving me with Carrie's large, unresponsive carcass. I squatted and then rolled her onto her side. Thelma returned with a dry towel, a short garbage bin, a roll of paper towels, and a damp washcloth. With the wet rag, I removed most of the puke from Carrie's face and chest. Her eyes fluttered awake and her mouth opened and closed like a fish pulled from water. She chewed her tongue for several seconds and then slurred, "Ssssorry." I managed to assist her from the house to the passenger seat of Thelma's El Camino. I propped Carrie up with her seat belt, lowered the passenger window, and left her with an empty grocery bag in case she felt sick again. Then I went back inside to clean up the living room.

I had to park in Carrie's front yard and wait for her to sober up enough to climb the cinderblock steps into her trailer. When I returned to the house late that afternoon, I found Thelma watching television on her loveseat, eating the Meals on Wheels lunch I had brought home to her earlier.

I approached her slowly.

Without taking her eyes off the TV, she stabbed some cold green beans off the foam plate and shoved them into her mouth.

"You get Carrie home safe?"

I replied with a curt yes. I squeezed my hands into fists.

"Good."

I waited for a thank you. It didn't come. I snatched the plate from Thelma's hands, walked to the kitchen, and dumped the food into the sink.

The Old Lady squinted at me curiously.

"That's a waste, boy."

I began to yell. I can't remember everything I said, but I know I called Thelma selfish. I called her a burden on my granduncle and I asked her why she couldn't try to emulate his behavior. I repeated some of the things the people at church had said about her, what they said about the company she kept, and how unfair it was for Thelma to inconvenience my granduncle by bringing bad people into his home.

The Old Lady coughed and turned her head back towards the television screen.

"Careful, boy," she sighed. "It's just as easy to find the devil in church."

That evening, I tried to avoid Thelma. My granduncle came home and I explained to him what had happened. He said he didn't need a sixteen-year-old kid to speak for him. He demanded I apologize to his sister, but didn't insist any further after I refused. I confined myself to my granduncle's side of the house and skipped dinner.

I usually slept in the room next to Thelma's, but to ensure I didn't see her, I decided to spend the night on a chaise lounge by the glass doors to the rear patio.

My granduncle gave me a thin blanket and a pillow.

I fell asleep staring out into the backyard. The dark grass resembled deep water. I imagined the flash of lightning bugs to be signal flares.

$\sim \sim \sim \sim$

I woke in the dark to a chorus of singing cicadas, chirping crickets, and a soft but urgent tapping on the glass behind me. I rolled over to see a solid shadow pressed against the transparent door. In those few seconds after waking, I found it difficult to distinguish dream from reality. I felt no apprehension rising to my feet and moving closer to determine what the shadow wanted.

I unlocked the door, and with the click of the sliding deadbolt the static shadow rushed into the house and tossed me backwards onto the chaise lounge. The shadow grabbed my shirt. Its claws scratched my chest. It ran its stinking talons across my face and spoke in trebly whispers. With foul breath, it asked for help. It needed whatever I had to give. It dragged its nails down my belly.

I closed my eyes tight with fear.

My granduncle's voice came. The claws vanished and I peeked through my eyelids to see him standing above, gripping the shadow's wrists, pushing the specter out the door.

"Not tonight," he said.

But the shadow persisted. It apologized, it asked for something, anything, he could provide. It would do whatever my granduncle liked, what it knew he liked, for whatever he could spare from his wallet.

The moving silhouette sounded familiar, but not until I heard my granduncle murmur, "Another night," did I identify the shadow as one of Thelma's frequent guests, Boo.

The door locked.

"You okay, Donald?"

I didn't know. I had a few scratches but I sensed a deeper injury I couldn't yet articulate.

"I'm fine."

He asked me if I wanted to finish sleeping in my own room, but I said no.

"I'm fine," I said.

"Okay," he panted. "Okay then."

My granduncle gently squeezed my shoulder and then retired to his bedroom.

His words repeated in my head: Not tonight, another night. Not tonight? As in tomorrow, or the next day, as in other nights, other instances, regular occurrences?

Later I would learn to recognize my granduncle's history of using desperate women for sex. I'd finally acknowledge that he had very many children with several different women. I'd admit that my granduncle had caused others immeasurable pain and suffering, and confront his failure to show his sons and daughters the financial and emotional support he showed me, and I would eventually have to concede to myself that I didn't know how to love him any less.

Trying to return to sleep on my granduncle's chair, my temples thumped and flushed with blood. I could feel my heart implode as I choked on my own saliva. Hot tears stung the tiny scratches on my dry cheeks.

I started to regret the spiteful words I had said earlier to the Old Lady, recalling an episode of *Springer* titled "Christmas with the Klan" where Jerry says, "I am struck by how easy so many of us call ourselves a particular religion...giving little thought to it other than, well, that's what my parents are and we celebrate certain holidays...In God's eyes we are not defined merely by what we call ourselves...We are what we are based on how we behave... when nobody's watching but God."

Springer's sentiments echoed a maxim Thelma had repeated to me since I first learned to walk, "Boy, pay no attention to what a person says. Watch what they do."

I had made a mistake believing that some had earned a holy right to cast aspersions onto others, wrong in supposing one could ascertain another person's value through secondhand knowledge or brief glimpses into their lives. I can't sort all those I encounter among the good and the bad. Considering how much I have yet to understand about myself, how can I assume to know everything about anyone else?

~ ~ ~ ~

The coffin closes and my granduncle grabs the opposite end of the casket. With the help of two of the funeral directors we hoist Thelma's body and begin the careful journey through the front doors of the church, down the sandy red-brick steps and sidewalk, to the white hearse waiting to carry her to the cemetery in Society Hill.

Exiting the church, the bright summer sky blinds me. We slide Thelma's casket into the cab of the vehicle and my eyes adjust. I think I see Boo standing at the far end of the parking lot in her stained dress and matted wig. I imagine she has come from the crack dealer's on the corner of Sixth and Washington Street. Hindered by a sense of curiosity or respect for the dead, she has never appeared so still. She casts a brilliant glow as her sweating skin sparkles in the sun.

I'm reminded that people have complexity and duality, not unlike an exploitive tabloid talk show allowing individuals largely unrepresented in mainstream media to share their experiences. I offer an inaudible prayer for Boo before heading towards the cars lining up for the funeral procession. I'll try to keep an eye out for her whenever I'm in the neighborhood. I wish her the best and that she never goes overlooked or unheard for too long.

~ ~ ~ ~

My family follows the hearse to the burial site. In the car, my mother, granduncle, Dorothy May, and I ride in silence. We travel down 151 and then north on Highway 15. The open pit of earth that will become Thelma's grave rests in a large glade behind a decaying AME church. Thelma's parents are buried there alongside my granduncle's first wife.

Bordered by trees and dense brush, the only clear entrance onto the cemetery grounds features a slender gravel road barely wide enough for a car. The hearse squeezes through the path and the rest of the convoy parks beside the church. We get out and follow the tire tracks trenched into the dirt and rocks.

The thick foliage forms a tunnel around us, and at the end shines the light from the clearing. A tearful Dorothy May strides up to me. She breaks her somber quiet to tell me she liked the eulogy I gave and that it had made her feel closer to Thelma. At the memorial, I had spoken about the Old Lady's proclivity for profanity and chain-smoking, her tendency to speak openly about bodily functions, and her violent temper whenever someone didn't show her respect. I had mentioned how some considered her a difficult woman. I had also shared examples of her courage and compassion, her kindness, and the responsibility she felt for others. I had noticed Dorothy May and my mother in the front row smiling together through tears.

In the years preceding Thelma's death, my mother had retired and moved to Hartsville in order to care for her mother, the Old Lady. A few months following my mother's move south, Thelma made a significant revelation. She confirmed that my mother had a secret sister.

My mother explained this to me on the phone, "Mama gave birth to another daughter, Dorothy May."

"What?"

"While her husband was fighting in Korea, Mama slept with one of his friends and she got pregnant."

"Like an episode of *Springer*," I replied calmly.

"Yes, I guess. Lord, have mercy. She gave Dorothy May to a distant cousin to raise in Florida. Mama says she tried to get Dorothy May back after separating from my father but the cousin refused."

"Are you okay, Mom?"

"What do you mean?"

"This is a lot to learn. Are you upset?"

"At who, Mama? Mama's daughter? Who can I be angry at? Who would you be angry at?"

"I don't know."

"I'm just shocked. I'm tired. If I was younger I might be more emotional about this. Mama will never say sorry anyway. You know how she is."

When Thelma got sick and her pneumonia grew serious, my mother called Dorothy May. I wish Dorothy May had reached her mother's bedside in time. I wish she had had the chance to say goodbye to the Old Lady. I like to envision Thelma pushing away the tubes flowing in and out of her body, raising her weak head from her starched hospital pillow to tell her daughters to take care of themselves and each other.

Standing beside the grave with my head bowed in prayer, I think of a line from Jerry Springer's Final Thought in the episode "Springer Sex Circus" featuring comic-hypnotist Denny More: "Why can't there be levels of existence or communication beyond human comprehension or levels which some people have a better knack of reaching than others?"

This notion comforts me as I turn away from Thelma's resting place. Maybe she could exist again somewhere else. Maybe I might learn to speak to her in a different way.

I extend an elbow to my mother and she takes hold of me. I guide her up the incline of the short gravel road back to the parked cars. My grand-uncle and my new aunt follow closely to ensure no one slips or trips to the ground. The summer sun peeks through the canopy of leaves and slaps our backs like a warm, friendly palm.

THE ANIMALS WE INVENT

Thursday, September 22, 2011—An hour after the arrest, phone calls from South Hartsville flood city hall. These citizens have faced harassment, detention, and accusation because of a lie.

They want answers.

I introduce myself. "I'm the public information officer. How may I help you?"

The callers protest. I listen quietly. I share their frustrations.

When they fall silent, tired and waiting for me to respond, I carefully recite the statement I've prepared: "We don't want to dwell on this crime. This matter will be settled in court. It is not for us to judge, to condone, or to condemn."

Feeling dismissed, most people hang up their phones.

But one man does not relent.

He asks me, "Do you know how many times cops stopped me over this mess at Jack Be Nimble? How many times my son was stopped?"

"Our thoughts are with all those affected, truly. The city is also thankful for the tireless efforts demonstrated by many members of our local law enforcement."

In the weeks immediately following the fire and alleged theft at Jack Be Nimble, I heard of white officers storming through Southside accosting black men. City officials saw a surge in complaints about law enforcement and reports of misconduct, intimidation, and verbal attacks. Downtown, in the vicinity of the crime, police increased patrols. Walking around unaccompanied by a white person often subjected me to questioning. Returning to my car after a late movie showing, a pair of officers approached me. One officer asked if I owned the vehicle. I said yes. He asked for my name, and when I gave it to them the other cop smiled in recognition. He tapped his partner and said, "That's the boy that writes for the mayor." They let me leave without having to show identification, and a mix of resentment, gratitude, and guilt covered me like a heavy coat.

The man on the phone laughs. "They've gotten you, brother."

"Excuse me?"

He asks, "Are you black?"

"What?"

"Aren't you angry?"

"What do you want me to say, sir?"

"The city owes the black community an apology!"

"We will not apologize, sir."

"We?"

"I can't apologize, sir."

I hear a click in the receiver and then the dial tone. Pressing the handset harder to my ear, I listen to the airy pitch become a howl.

For Immediate Release:

911 CALL LEADS TO DISCOVERY OF ROBBERY AND ARSON

Hartsville, SC—Wednesday evening, January 26th, 2011, Hartsville city police and firefighters received a 911 call for help at the 100 block of East Carolina Avenue. When authorities arrived, they saw smoke coming from Jack Be Nimble, a children's clothing boutique. Police officers gained entry to the building where they discovered a fire and a person lying inside on the floor. They pulled the victim to safety and firefighters contained the flames. The victim was transported to an area hospital and is being treated for non-life-threatening injuries.

Darlington County sheriff's office crime scene units were called to the location. At this time Hartsville city police officials say two black male suspects entered the store shortly after dark, robbed and assaulted the victim, and then set fire to the building.

"This is a blatant disregard for human life and property, and justice will be served," said the Hartsville city manager. "I have all the confidence that our city police officials will get to the bottom of this heinous act."

This crime is currently under investigation. If you have any information regarding this case, you are asked to call the Hartsville Police Department or your local law enforcement agency.

CHAINS

A coalition of local pastors working with friends and family of the victim organized a prayer chain a few days after the crime. Over a thousand people lined up along Carolina Avenue, shoulder to shoulder, covering the two city blocks from Sixth Street to Fourth. State senators, members of city council, and the city manager stood among those gathered. I had a spot near the intersection of Fourth Street and Carolina, five buildings down from the charred remains of Jack Be Nimble.

Preachers positioned themselves every few yards to lead their section of the chain in prayer. The ministers signaled each other. Heads bowed, dropping in a wave down the sidewalk. I lowered my chin to my chest, closed my eyes, and reached for the hands of the strangers to my right and left. The holy man nearest to me began to pray. He asked God for solidarity. He pleaded for swift justice and mercy for the souls responsible for such a heinous act.

While the pastor recited scripture, I recalled the orange haze that had shrouded the same block nights earlier. The light from the streetlamps had bounced off smoke billowing from a blackened storefront. I remembered the smell of burning plastic tickling my throat. Firefighters pushed back spectators and residents evacuated from the adjoining buildings. I inched closer, peering fearfully at emergency medical technicians kneeling around a pale body draped in a white sheet. The memory is mute. I can't remember hearing anything over the sound of blood rushing to my skull.

Finally, the minister pleaded for Jesus's intercession and said amen. I released my neighbors' hands and wiped my sweaty palms on the sides of my pants. One of the strangers, a greying white woman, leaned in to hug me.

"Peace be with you," she sighed into my ear.

"And also with you," I replied.

She let me go. We smiled and nodded at one another, and then I turned away to walk home.

The line scattered. I moved with the groups heading east towards Third Street. Cutting between people and cars, I overhead someone say, "We'll catch them. We'll show those animals."

I realized I hadn't seen any other young black men in the prayer chain.

After I reached my house, I sat on the front steps thinking about "those animals" and what made them less than human. A police cruiser rolled past. I quickly rose to my feet and went inside.

RENDERINGS

I volunteered to distribute police sketches of three black men wanted for questioning. The posters described them as potential witnesses but many saw accomplices. Some of the shop owners downtown believed the men in these illustrations might have served as lookouts. Rumors spread. Some speculated at least five were involved in the attack on Jack Be Nimble.

People said, "They picked her place because they knew she would be in the store alone after dark. They had it all planned out, the animals."

I wondered if I had ever seen the faces on the poster skulking around the block. Maybe at the coffee shop I frequented. Did I ever see these men standing outside beneath the awning, sipping from steaming cups while considering the high-end kids' clothing store next door and how much cash might be inside?

I spent time studying the police flier. In the illustrations, one man had neat shoulder-length dreadlocks. Another had a short fade. These two faces looked familiar, but I couldn't identify them. The last man had more discernible features, sharp cheekbones and a wide jaw sloping forward to a pointed, cleft chin. A tiny crucifix dangled from his left ear. He wore a baseball hat low over his forehead and his eyes vanished below the bill.

I imagined his hidden gaze staring into my home between cracks in the blinds and curtains. I often envisioned narrowed greyscale pupils floating over me when I lay in bed. His image surfaced in my dreams.

For many weeks I couldn't stop searching the dark for the shark-like man in the fitted cap. And then one slow afternoon I entered the coffee shop beside the former Jack Be Nimble. The café looked empty except for a single barista standing behind the counter. She fiddled with the nozzles of an espresso machine, her back to the front door.

I approached the register and said hello. The barista turned around. She jumped.

Clutching her chest, she said I had startled her. I apologized and gave my order.

Before preparing my drink, she smiled and told me, "Be careful. The boys they're looking for look a lot like you."

I glanced over at the police poster taped to the window of the front door.

I couldn't see my resemblance in the ashen faces.

Days later, I stopped imagining the police drawings in places I felt vulnerable.

HISTORY

In October of 1994, while my mom attended a funeral, I spent time with my grandmother at Wash Tub Laundry on Fifth Street in Hartsville. I had wanted to be outside riding bikes with my cousins instead of watching daytime soap operas on ceiling-mounted televisions. My grandmother removed a load from one of the large dryers and dropped the warm clothes into a rolling laundry cart. She pushed the cart over to a clear table and ordered me to help her fold. While we worked, she tried to explain the plotlines on *The Young and the Restless*.

"You see him, with the mustache?" she said raising her chin in the direction of the nearest screen. "That's Victor Newman. He's a handsome white man. Him and Chuck Norris on *Walker, Texas Ranger*."

I ran a finger over my smooth upper lip.

During commercial breaks, advertisements for the nightly news played clips of Susan Smith crying for the return of her children. "I just can't express it enough, we just got to get them home. That's just where they belong, with their momma and their daddy."

I didn't understand why I couldn't play outdoors or how my freedom related to two missing children I had never met. I pleaded with my grandmother to let me leave the laundromat. Again, she said no.

"It's not safe for black boys to be riding around until they catch the man that took that white woman's children or she confesses to having taken those kids out herself."

"But I'm nine, Old Lady."

"You think they care? Shit. They were putting children younger than you on slave ships. Ask your daddy, he's from Ghana."

"That was a long time ago."

She stopped folding to remove a crumpled paper towel from the pocket of her ratty stretch pants. She pulled the Winston butt from her lips, tucked the cigarette and its fading embers into the wrinkled napkin, and crushed it in her fist. A final wisp of smoke rose from between her fingers.

She leaned close to whisper to me, "It was only two decades ago, right down the road in Lamar, a hundred white folks showed up at a schoolhouse and turned over a bus full of black children. They didn't care if they were kids. Black is black. Not a one of those people saw any real time in jail. They're still out here, walking around. They never went anywhere, they still own everything, and who knows what they've raised their children to believe. They'll treat you like a dog. Shit, a dog's life may mean more to them."

The Old Lady reached for the lighter and Winstons she kept in the breast pocket of her jean jacket. She lit a new cigarette, breathed deeply, and continued folding.

"White people get funny when they think their women are under attack. You ever hear of Rosewood?"

"No, Old Lady."

"'Cause they don't want you to know. A town in Florida made up of freed slaves. One white girl claims a black man hurt her and the town is burned to the ground, people are hanged, all strange fruit. They're serious about their women."

We continued folding in silence. We finished as the saxophone squeals of *The Bold and the Beautiful* theme song filled the laundromat. I didn't bother asking to go outside again.

For Immediate Release:

SLED CONTINUES JACK BE NIMBLE INVESTIGATION

Hartsville, SC—The Hartsville Police Department will turn over its examination into the assault and arson which occurred at Jack Be Nimble earlier this year. The South Carolina Law Enforcement Division will continue the investigation with needed assistance from the Hartsville Police Department. The Hartsville Chamber of Commerce is still offering $25,000 to anyone who can provide information leading to the arrest of the two suspects involved.

The city manager closed the door to our offices and locked it behind her. She sat in the chair across from my desk. Slouching down in the seat, she stared up vacantly. Her eyes scanned the water-spotted ceiling tiles and the insect carcasses trapped between the sheaths of the fluorescent lights.

After a few silent seconds she sighed. "This is going to hurt our relationship with the black community," she said.

A blinking cursor waited on my computer screen. I counted the expectant flashes, unsure how to begin filling the white space.

"Our relationship?" I said.

"The city and black people, yes."

"Probably." I punched down on the keys—*For Immediate Release: HARTSVILLE MOVING FORWARD AFTER JACK BE NIMBLE ARREST.*

She groaned. "The men the owner described for those sketches never existed. It's like Susan Smith in Union. How are people expected to move forward together when stuff like this keeps happening?"

My pinky ricocheted off Return...*was arrested and charged in connection to the assault and arson which occurred at Jack Be Nimble on January 26th, 2011... arrest was made by the South Carolina Law Enforcement Division (SLED)...*

"Did the profilers tell you when SLED will take her into custody?" I asked.

"No, they didn't tell me when. Did you talk to the mayor?"

"Yeah." *Hartsville's mayor issued a statement: "Despite the shock and anger, these events succeeded in helping to unite a community. This city witnessed outpourings of love, people banding together in their resolve to make our streets safer, and this is what we should focus on. My hope is we will continue to hold on to that commitment to our city because the only way we can move forward is together."*

The city manager sat up in her seat. She watched me for a moment. "Are you mad?"

"Why?"

"You knew her."

"I thought I did."

"Do you still believe her? Even after everything SLED has on her?"

"Doesn't matter if I believe her or not."

"Not really, but do you?"

"I don't know."

The city manager stood. She told me to finish the press release and have it ready to send out whenever SLED made the arrest. Before the city manager exited the room she asked, "Why did she have to say they were black?"

I typed, *Because America, because of its long history of violence towards people of color in response to perceived attacks on white femininity, because of Florida's Rosewood Massacre in 1923, because she knew there would be many ready to believe her, people ready to be validated in their belief that people with my skin color are animals.*

I held Delete and shrugged.

CLUES

In the weeks waiting for law enforcement to arrest the owner of Jack Be Nimble, I searched for earlier indications of her culpability. I tried to consolidate the person I knew with notes from the profiler's investigation. The image of the kind woman with the round face who had ordered cheaper editions for me at the college bookstore was reshaped by "conclusive with self-inflicted wounds." A person I chatted with regularly at chamber of commerce functions, a demure and devoted mother and wife who had started her own business, a person whose persistent grin never revealed how much debt threatened to crush her and her family, transformed, reinvented in response to "an absence of DNA evidence" and failed polygraph tests.

Like animals, humans can become especially vicious if they feel trapped or afraid. Does she remain a victim, guilty or innocent, if not a victim of the crimes she says she has endured, then a victim of her own hopelessness? I began to understand that there exists truth in what I see and what I do not see, and I had to acknowledge the limits of my perception. I began to accept that I might never understand how she felt in that moment, real or imagined.

~ ~ ~ ~

Thursday, September 22, 2011—The WPDE reporter watches her cameraman clip the tiny microphone to the lapel of my blazer. I'm thankful I didn't wear a striped shirt this morning, but disappointed I didn't have the foresight to shave.

The reporter smiles slyly, "The mayor didn't seem happy to see me in your office. He stamped out of here pretty fast. He doesn't trust you to speak on the arrest?"

"He trusts me. He's just curious why I've agreed to talk with you when we've already released a statement."

The mayor, the city manager, and the new police chief have all refused to appear on television. I have said yes, and the reporter doesn't ask me why. Perhaps she worries I might consider the risk of embarrassment and change my mind. If she did ask, I'd answer honestly—I have something to say about refusing to be victimized by fear. I want to share what I'm learning about the capacity of grace, and the difficult but empowering work of allowing myself to forgive without forgetting. Because if I wait for the pain I witness to be validated with an apology, resentment will tear into my body like sharp, dirty fangs to snap my bones. If she asked, I'd tell the reporter the same thing I told the mayor: my position includes relaying important messages to citizens, and the news camera offers me a venue to do my job better.

Instead, she asks me if I know what I'm going to say. I tell her I plan to repeat the sentiments expressed in the press release.

She smiles again. "You know I have to ask about your officers? There were a lot of complaints about their search for suspects and the way the former police chief handled things before he retired."

"Some say he did too much; some say he did too little. I don't know much about it, I wasn't full-time yet." The cameraman turns on the wireless transmitter and hands it to me. I fasten it to my belt. "We were very grateful to have Interim Chief Thompson serve us and now we have Chief Hudson who expresses a real commitment to community-oriented policing. The city supports local law enforcement and the fine work done daily by so many of our officers."

I repeat this once the camera comes on. My validation of area cops leads the six o'clock news and airs again at eleven. The mayor texts me around midnight to say I did well.

The city manager thanks me when I enter her office the following morning.

I approach her desk.

"I'm surprised to see you," she says. "I thought you might want to quit after all the calls yesterday."

"Nope."

She says I looked good on television. She liked what I said during the interview about our responsibility as human beings: to seek compassion, to demand more than good enough, and to celebrate sincere efforts to improve.

She reminds me there will be more calls today.

I tell her I know.

I turn to exit the room, and she says, "Sorry."

Startled by the earnestness in her voice, I stop moving.

"Why are you apologizing? You didn't do anything wrong."

"Yes, I know," she says. "I just thought someone should say it."

IN OTHER WORDS

I imagine P will struggle to provide an easy answer when customers ask about our imminent departure. Why, after only two and a half years of successful operation, would we choose to sell our Thai restaurant and leave America? Where to begin explaining the impetus spurring us to go in search of an uncertain future in another country, deserting the life we've built?

I have yet to fully articulate my reasons for making the move, and I believe some of my motivations remain unknown even to me.

When people ask, I'll probably give an explanation about cultivating experiences to supplement my writing. I'll tell them P has decided to return to Thailand to take charge of her father's auto-parts business. These justifications greatly simplify our decision and satisfy most people's curiosity.

But I wonder what P will consider telling folks when they ask her.

Would she say, *We're tired of treading water and struggling to barely stay ahead of our debts from the mortgage on our house, the car payments, the student loans, and the other things we've needed to help us stay afloat in the United States?* Would she mention, *The cost of living in Thailand is much lower?* Would she tell them about the number of sleepless nights spent fretting over money and how *regularly, I notice Donald eyeing me like an open fire exit to escape a burning theater?*

Or maybe P will describe the night we first spoke earnestly about going...*A few months ago, Donald storms into the kitchen raving about a rude patron. This is common. If there isn't a city government function or meeting he has to attend as the public information officer, Donald usually comes to the restaurant in the evenings to help out or do some writing at one of the open tables. A lot of times he witnesses customers say or do things he finds unacceptable and he gets angry. Once, he caught a diner searching behind the checkout counter for a way to turn off the music playing in our restaurant. When confronted, the person calmly explained that they didn't like jazz and then asked if there was any way she could connect her phone to our speakers because she had a better playlist.*

Donald addressed her politely. He apologized and told her no.

After she left, Donald punched a hole through the door of our stock room.

On another occasion, a satisfied customer asked to speak with me—to give his compliments to the chef. I didn't want to come to the front but Donald insisted. The diner was impressed I was a woman. He congratulated me for doing such a fine job and said it tasted very authentic. The customer didn't acknowledge my nationality or care to ask about my years of experience studying and preparing Thai cuisine. He told me he had spent several months in Southeast Asia, and then gave me some instructions on how to improve the taste of my tom yum.

I thanked the patron for his feedback. Once he had gone, Donald kicked the industrial fryer so hard we had to call someone to repair it.

So like I said, Donald comes into the kitchen in a rage. I am flipping and stirring noodles on the wok for an order of pad see ew. Donald slams his fist against the door of the commercial refrigerator and I point a hot spatula at his face. I tell him to relax. Our manager appears beside him. I ask her to explain what happened while Donald continues to pace and grunt.

She tells me a white guy ordered a panang curry at level five spicy. One of our waiters had warned him, but the guy insisted he could handle it. He said he wanted his food "as hot as Thais eat." The dude got the curry, took a sip from his spoon, and said he couldn't eat it. It was too spicy. Duh. He ordered a second thing, a pepper steak. This time the manager interceded to tell him it's pretty hot as well. He dismissed her advice, got it anyway, and, big surprise, it was too spicy. Finally, he forced himself to settle on something mild and he devoured half of a broccoli stir-fry. When he got the bill charging him for the three menu items, he refused to pay.

At this point in her account, P might choose to exclude details of how I exploded into a rant about the rampant sense of entitlement and narcissism in America, egotism stemming from a national identity founded on protecting and catering to privilege while decreeing that individual freedoms are more important than empathy for others. Scooping the pad see ew noodles from the bowl-shaped frying pan, P told me not to use generalizations. She poured the meal onto a curved, white plate set on top of the wok range. Carrying the dish to a stainless steel prep table, she reminded me that narcissists exist everywhere and self-importance is not exclusive to the Western Hemisphere. She tapped a small desk bell to signal for a member of the wait staff to deliver the order.

I ask the manager what happened after the customer refused to pay, but Donald interjects. Donald says he bargained with the patron. The customer paid half the bill and the restaurant covered the rest. Donald looks defeated after he finishes telling me, more beaten than he usually does when we lose money.

I ask him what's wrong, and he stares up at the kitchen exhaust hood and exhales loudly.

He says, "Why do I stay in this country?"

I ask him what he means, assuming he's just being dramatic—Donald is very dramatic.

He says, "I could live somewhere else."

I told him nothing is stopping him. He's an American. He has a passport. He can basically go, and stay, anywhere he wishes.

He says, "Okay, let's go."

Now, this surprises me. He's made flippant comments about expatriating ever since we first met, like whenever he gets annoyed with some aspect of his life in the US. But he has started saying things like this more frequently, and each time he threatens to emigrate he sounds more believable.

I ask the manager to take charge of the kitchen, and then I lead Donald through a pair of swinging doors into a service hallway behind the galley. In her description, P might omit some sensory details. The dark, slender corridor lined with empty produce delivery boxes. Weeks had passed since the fluorescent bulbs in the ceiling lights had burned out, and neither P nor I had remembered to replace them. A glowing red EXIT sign suspended above the rear entrance door at the end of the hall silhouetted P in the dim, tight space.

I tell Donald I want to know if he is serious about wanting to leave the country. I say, "This isn't like moving to another state. This is a much bigger commitment." Donald has to be sure.

I ask him where this urge came from. He starts by talking about his job. He tells me he mostly loves the work because he gets to help people and serve the community. But always being on call to draft statements whenever a crisis appears has begun giving him anxiety. Also, his position as a bridge between government and citizens often makes him a target for people's frustrations with public policy and local politics. As he says this, I remember the week police arrested one of the business owners on the same block as my restaurant for torching her own children's clothing store. Donald received a bunch of calls and angry emails. People came into his office yelling, demanding an apology for how some local authorities conducted the investigation.

Donald says he yearns to help people another way while following his own passions and conscience. He wants to focus more energy on his creative writing. Sure, whatever, but I ask him what he would do to make money. He reveals to me he has already begun looking into teaching positions at universities in Bangkok.

Moving to Thailand would make my family immensely happy, and a huge part of me has always wanted to return.

P asked me if I had any more reasons.

She said wanting to quit my job was not enough.

He talks about his conflict with his home. Donald says when customers do stuff like the patron who tried to avoid paying the bill earlier, it is hard not to feel like it's a part of something else, something systemic, a lineage of oppression that frames so many of his daily interactions. Donald must always consider that some customers might demand more from our restaurant, or behave differently in our establishment, because we are an Asian woman and a black man. If Donald gets into a dispute with a white customer, there is an underlying context: "People who look like you once held people who look like me in bondage." This is especially true here in a small southern town like Hartsville, South Carolina, where Donald's great-grandfather was born as a slave.

I admit to him that I could never fully understand how that feels, having been born in Thailand into the ruling class.

Donald asks why I chose to come to the United States and why I've stayed.

P quietly considered the question, and for a moment we could hear the manager asking the dishwasher to help prepare some fresh spring rolls.

I came for an education. In school, Americans are encouraged to think for themselves and ask questions. They learn to challenge ideas and share their opinions. I stay because I really like that the USA has laws meant to protect people's rights to say whatever they want, even if it's offensive.

I also like that there is mass infrastructure. The fact that I live in a rural area with a population under eight thousand and have access to clean, drinkable tap water and reliable electricity with Wi-Fi is incredible. I remind Donald that for many in Thailand, and Ghana, where his dad is from, this would seem impossible.

I go on: There is a lot of diversity, and some mainstream media reflects that diversity. In Thailand, I've never seen any of the country's many ethnic minorities on network television. And then I talk about the diversity of food in America. I love how a dish or recipe can carry and continue the traditions of the culture from which it originated. A meal can express a story about an entire population. America is a buffet where I can taste and know more cultures, and meet foods and people I never knew existed. This exposure has made me a better cook.

I nodded, but P couldn't see my acknowledgment in the dark.

Donald doesn't say anything for what seems like forever. A thought comes into my head: Maybe he should live outside of the country for a while. All he can see right now are the bad things. Distance will give him perspective like it did for me.

I tell him I'm aware of the debt and the consumerism, and the racism, sexism, and classism, but I never regret coming to the US. America has many problems and often fails to meet its own standards, but America is a home to me—where I first had a real chance to find myself—and I love it still.

I silently repeated what P had said about finding herself in America. I realized that a large part of me wanted the same. I yearned to go abroad in order to find myself beyond the classification of my race and nationality. I wanted an opportunity to live in a place where I might move beyond the limits of myself.

Before I could convey this to her, P spoke again.

Finally, I ask him why he wants to move elsewhere when our life here is good.

He says he wants to try for better.

I say, "Going somewhere else doesn't guarantee you'll be happier or more satisfied." In Thailand, he will experience different debts, new prejudices, and oppressive social constructs and hierarchies.

And he says he understands that, but over there he might also experience new freedom.

I reached for P, fumbling across her forearms and wrists before cupping her hands in mine.

"Okay," I tell him. "We'll go."

P slapped my belly. She stepped away and pushed through the swinging doors into the bright light of the kitchen. I lingered in the hallway a little longer, listening to the quick, restless thumping of my heart, envisioning in the shadows all we would have to do to prepare for our journey.

There are a couple new orders waiting for me when Donald and I finish talking. I walk over to the sink, wash my hands, and then approach the wok range. I turn up the gas for the burner and watch the flames grow taller.

I think about what's next. My father wants to retire soon and he has an idea to start a second auto-parts distribution business in Bangkok. It's not cooking, but I'm sure I can manage.

If this prompts people to ask P why she would agree to sacrifice her aspirations, I know she will correct them. *I'm not abandoning my dream of having a restaurant—I've wanted this since I was a kid. I will have another restaurant, maybe in Thailand or again in the States if we decide to return. But I think it would be good for my family and me, and for Donald too. I know what Donald is talking about, even if he isn't certain how to say it yet. I recognize the longing to discover a newer world and find the truest version of oneself. That desire brought me here, where I experienced my greatest isolation, fear, and confusion, and found so many good things. It's a gift, you know?*

It'll be interesting to see how Donald adjusts. It'll be fun to help guide him. As an American, Donald was born with boundless privileges, and many of these priv-ileges he may not realize until he resides beyond the borders of his home country.

Or maybe P wouldn't say any of this to a person with only a passing curiosity. Maybe, when people ask her why we are leaving, P might offer a brief response for the sake of expediency.

Because we have the chance.

JUNK

I follow the footpaths in the carpet, navigating through the mounds and walls of forgotten items. I carry a load of wrinkled dresses outside to P on the front porch. She has to take breaks about every half hour. The odor of the house—a heavy funk of urine and decomposition under a fog of disinfectant spray, bleach, and moth balls—gives her nausea and makes her head throb with pain.

"How can you stay in there so long?" she asks.

I bend to rest the load in a weather-battered patio chair.

"I'm used to it," I say. I recall for her a memory of a high school friend teasing me about my clothes always reeking of a blend between a hospital and museum.

P grins. "But it's gotten much worse since your grandmother died."

"True."

P's gloved hands grab one of the frocks from the chair. She turns away and begins to shake clumps of dust and rat shit from its creases. The gown still has a price tag hanging from its collar. I take a deep breath of clean air and reenter the house.

My mother calls to me. She has posted herself on the living room sofa to surveil our efforts.

"What was that you just took out of here?" she asks.

"Some outfits."

"Why didn't you let me look at them first?"

Yesterday, Mom and I argued over a dozen pairs of high heels. Her peripheral neuropathy makes it impossible for her to wear any shoes that can't provide enough room for her foot braces. But she still mulled over giving away the shoes. She examined each one carefully, running her fingers along the seams. Although the injections she receives to her eyes every six weeks have helped to slow the degeneration caused by her retinal vascular occlusions, her vision still suffers. She held each piece of footwear so close to her face she appeared to be sniffing their soles.

"Mom, we don't have time for you to look at every item we carry out of here."

Because in a few weeks P and I are moving abroad and don't know when or if we'll return, my mother has finally agreed to let us make her home more livable. I've requested additional garbage roll carts from the city's sanitation department, mapped a route to the nearest landfill, and contacted people at local thrift shops about coming to haul away items others might use. The cleaning has taken much longer than I expected. Mom has made the process more difficult, and even declared her bedroom off limits.

"You know emptying out this house is important, right? I won't be here if you trip or fall over something."

My mother flails her hands like she would to shoo a persistent fly. She hates when I use hypotheticals. She says I'm too negative.

"I'll be fine," she says. Mom points an elbow at me, a signal that she needs help to hoist herself onto her feet and cane. I assist her from the couch. After she finishes her brief groans, she tells me to call P inside. "Let's lock up the house and you two can drive me somewhere to eat."

Mom pats my scowling face. "My treat, baby."

~ ~ ~ ~

For my ninth birthday, I had a sleepover at my house with my only childhood friend. At one point during the evening my friend thoughtlessly opened the door to a closet on the first floor. Inside, a meter-high heap comprised of unopened boxes of mail-order products, trash bags filled with clothes never worn, print periodicals, random dishes and silverware, books, VHS tapes, and festive but nondenominational holiday decorations packed the confined space. I hurried to shut the door before the objects shifted and poured through the open entrance like a landslide.

I explained to my friend that my mother didn't like me looking in that room.

Confused by what he had found, his head tilted to the side. He said, "Your mom has a lot of junk."

I suddenly felt embarrassed. I wanted to apologize, but I wasn't sure why.

After returning my friend to his family's house the next day, I sat quietly in the back seat with my arms folded on the ride home. My mother, sensing something went wrong at the sleepover, asked if I enjoyed having my friend spend the night. I ignored the question and posed my own, "Why do you have so much stuff?"

My mother paused to think. In the rearview mirror, I could see a reflection of her eyes darting back and forth, reading over something invisible to make sure she understood the context.

"Did you let him go into the downstairs room?" Her tone had moved from concerned to threatening. My righteousness dissipated and I quickly uncrossed my arms and turned to look out the window. "Donnie, did you let him touch my things? I told you, I don't want you going through that room! I don't want you touching my things! They're mine!" Her voice grew louder as she continued to yell.

Minutes later, she calmed herself. She tried to rationalize the quantity in the downstairs closet. "We don't have a garage or shed for storage like other homes," she clarified.

I nodded like I understood although I hadn't. I didn't want her to scream again or smack me. So I didn't remind her how we had a basement and attic also filled with things, and how every hanging rod in every closet throughout the house had bowed or broken under the weight of the clothes we owned. I wanted to ask her why we had so much, and why our family of two could never find enough room to accommodate all our stuff. But I didn't want to argue.

I'd recall the same question as a teen, when my mother began the long process of emptying our home and getting the house ready for sale after she retired. We worked slowly against her reluctance to part with each item. Removing everything from the downstairs closet revealed that it was actually a restroom—a half bath with a toilet and a sink buried for decades.

"Why is there never enough room to accommodate all our stuff?" I ask myself again, aloud.

"What did you say?" P's inquiry is muffled through the protective mask covering her mouth and nose.

I shake my head dismissively and we continue to labor in silence.

She peels open an extra-large garbage bag and I reach for another stack of soiled, old newspapers.

~ ~ ~ ~

Since I first learned to read, I have known these words: Quality, Value, Convenience, and Shipping and Handling. They showed up on envelopes my mother pulled from the mailbox. They appeared on parcels that arrived at my mother's front door.

Curious one day, I opened one of these packages and found some gaudy jewelry she had bought by phone. Mom filled entire dresser drawers with items like these. Forged from fake gold and cubic zirconia, these affordable, shiny pieces adorned her hands, wrists, neck, and ears. She'd wear them even though they stained her fingers green and left rashes on her skin. She liked how the bling from these tiny treasures attracted stares from her co-workers and strangers. She liked how the jewelry made her harder to forget.

Often my mother would fall asleep bathed in the blue glow of the television screen, the volume barely loud enough to hear the enthusiastic oohs and ahs of actors in shopping channel infomercials. The products promised to solve problems my mother didn't know she had. She'd wake up needing the ThighMaster™, the EZ Cracker™, the Slap Chop™, Ginsu™ knives, the ShoeDini™, the Deluxe Gopher™, the Ab Roller™, the Veg-o-Matic™, the Miracle Thaw™ Defrosting Tray, the Magic Bullet®, the Ninja® Master Prep® Pro, three crockpots by Cook's Essentials®, a George Foreman® Grill, and more—much more.

My mother had to part with most of these items after she decided to retire from her career as a software engineer at a global telecommunications company. She planned to move to South Carolina and care for my grandmother, but all the stuff Mom had gathered over the years couldn't fit in a single twenty-six-foot moving truck.

But she managed to bring the Foreman Grill.

I find it in the kitchen under a small tower of crusty pots stacked on the counter beside the kitchen sink. I yank the grill from the bottom of the pile. Roaches scuttle as the pots bang and clang to the floor.

"What was that?" Mom hollers over the sound of P vacuuming in the living room.

There are shows on television about my mother's tendency to accumulate. In every episode the compulsion usually results from an unaddressed trauma. I suppose Mom likes to buy things because she can control what she purchases. She can hold onto her belongings until she decides to let go. Her possessions wouldn't disappear like her dad or the baby she lost during childbirth. The Foreman Grill, caked with years-old bacon grease, couldn't walk away like my father had with his new family.

"It's nothing!" I shout in response.

I slide open a window above the kitchen sink and chuck the Foreman Grill out into the yard. The appliance tumbles in the dry, unkempt grass before splitting on its hinges. The top half of the grill rests a few feet from my dead grandmother's rusted El Camino parked on the lawn.

~ ~ ~ ~

P joins me in the restroom where I'm on my knees trying to scrub the dark rings from my mother's bathtub. P pulls down her face mask to ask me, "Are you sure you can leave your mom?" And I remember sitting beside my mother in a family eye care office. The ophthalmologist looked like a kid in his oversized white lab coat. His small stature and timid persona made it difficult for him to carry such grave news. He sped through the details: a routine exam had revealed retinal hemorrhage and oracular degeneration. "I'm sorry ma'am," he said. "You're going blind."

I couldn't appreciate his brevity. Despite the succinctness of his diagnosis, its destruction crept over me slowly. Outside, the gushing summer rain mimicked my mother's tears. My mother leaned to cover one of my tight fists with a shaking hand. I wanted to open my fingers to squeeze her clammy, quivering palm. But I had become rock, a hard remnant of the world vanishing from her.

P reminds me that I can't remain the one on whom my mother most relies—her rock—when I no longer sit beside her.

"She'll be okay without me," I reply.

P sighs heavily, unconvinced.

I push and pull the coarse brush harder over the stained enamel. Streaks of brown suds creep towards the drain.

~ ~ ~ ~

Growing up, I kept my most cherished belongings in a travel trunk that had once belonged to my father. Every week, I would pull my favorite novels, comics, toys, and cassettes from the trunk and examine them carefully. I'd rank the contents and compare them with objects around my room.

I'd choose what to include or exclude. In the trunk I cultivated a space for only the best of my things, and it became a way for me to escape the clutter around me. This habit provided me a sense of gratification, and perhaps led to my affinity for packing.

When not cleaning my mother's house or meeting with her physicians, P and I pack for our move overseas. I hunt for boxes around town; I collect them from liquor stores and supermarkets, and snag a few flat-rate shipping packages from the post office.

I divide the cardboard containers by size and color. I give each box a subject and designation. I take pleasure in separating items, assigning them a place. I enjoy the sense of completion when I tape a box closed.

I might not be able to correct my mother's junk eyes or clear the mess from her home, but I can pack up my own life in a way that gives my existence order.

P comes home from a meeting with the buyers of our restaurant.

Everywhere there are open boxes.

"We can't take all of this, right?" She reaches for a box labeled BEST BOOKS 1 of 2 and shakes it.

"Careful," I say.

"This box is light." She cradles it in one arm and uses her house key to slice open the tape covering the folds. "There's only a few books in here."

"Yes," I say, tapping the words scrawled on the side in permanent marker. "Only the best ones." I point to another box that waits on the floor of our living room alongside a dozen others sealed and ready to mail. "That one has the other half of my favorite books."

P's eyes narrow in curiosity or frustration. She asks me why I don't combine the two boxes in a bigger box or include other things we might need in Thailand. She suggests I fill the empty space in the box with underwear or shirts instead of bubble wrap.

I recoil at the idea.

"Why not?" she asks.

"Because books and under clothes don't fit together."

P laughs. "So what?"

"I just don't like it. It's not organized."

I try to snatch the box, but P steps backwards.

"Quist," she says forcefully.

I tug hard and her nails drag across the dry cardboard, making me cringe.

The box slips from her grip, dumping my books to the floor.

I kneel. Grumbling to myself, I inspect each book carefully before returning it to the box.

P stands above me, watching.

"What?" I snap at her without looking up from packing.

"Donald?" she says.

I hate the pity in her voice.

She doesn't have to tell me you can't keep everything. I already know. I've repeated those words for weeks.

I raise my head and breathe slowly, "Okay."

Okay, I'll make sure to use every square inch of this box for what I really want and need.

Okay, we'll donate the majority of my books to the public library.

We'll have a yard sale and give what we don't sell to friends and local charities.

I'll learn to let stuff go.

~ ~ ~ ~

Mom leans forward and her face expands on the screen of my phone. "I can see you, baby!" she exclaims. Below her floating head, a tiny window displays my own pixelated reflection. I look tired but I mirror my mother's broad grin.

She asks me about my flight.

"It was long, over twenty hours."

This reminds us of the severity of the distance, the impossibility of me reaching her quickly on the other side of the Earth.

We observe each other quietly for several seconds.

I ask about her journey back to South Carolina from Washington Dulles International Airport.

P and I had wanted to say goodbye to my father and stepmother before we left the United States, so we rented a car to drive from South Carolina to Maryland where he lives. Despite my objections, Mom insisted she come too. Dad had agreed to drop P and me off at Dulles, and take my mother to Union Station in Washington, D.C., where she'd catch the Silver Service/Palmetto Amtrak train heading south. But the morning of our flight my father changed his mind. He called hours before our boarding call to say he couldn't chauffer us around. He said he needed to work and wished me good luck in Thailand.

While P stood at a kiosk beside the baggage claim trying to procure a shuttle service to escort my mother to the train station, Mom listed the ways we would stay connected—texts, emails, social network messages, and weekly online video chats. She enumerated the things we would do the next time I came home.

As my mother spoke, I studied the distinctions of her face: the smile lines, the folds around her cloudy eyes, and the scar on her forehead she had received as a little girl from some vicious schoolboys with air rifles.

The digital glow of electronic devices would flatten and smooth these intimate features.

Suddenly, her enthusiastic chatter broke into soft sobs. I drew her into a tight hug. I cried too, nuzzling my damp cheek against the top of her head.

I whispered an apology, "I'm sorry for leaving...but I need to."

I pulled back from the embrace and she told me in a shaky voice not to worry. She promised to take care of herself. She said she would keep the house clean. She would see me again.

I made a promise too. I said I'll be away but I won't be gone. I will not disappear and I will not throw her away.

P and I left her at the large sliding doors leading to the parking lot. My mother's driver seemed kind. He carried her suitcase outside to the passenger van and then returned to wait with her while she watched P and me shuffle towards our terminal.

I peered over my shoulder for a glimpse of my mother. I saw her pressing her weight forward onto her cane. Squinting hard in my direction, she tried to keep sight of me among all the other blurry moving objects cutting across her pupils.

"You made it home safely?" I say to my phone, and my mother's cyber doppelganger nods. "Caught the train okay? Someone picked you up from Florence?"

"Yes. Your granduncle was there waiting at the train station. I told you. I'll be fine."

"You better."

Mom doesn't speak for a while. She gazes at me, grinning again.

And I can't stop myself from smiling too.

"I see you, baby," she says.

"I see you too."

TO THAT / TO FIND, AND NOT TO YIELD :
LOG II

CARTOGRAPHY

START AT WAT ARUN (TEMPLE OF DAWN)

Climb the large stone steps to the center tower. Careful. The stairs from the second landing are steep. The rock is smooth, and it's easy to slip with sweating hands. There is a single metal rail, rusted red, wrapped in rope. It offers some grip. Pull yourself onto the next level.

Look up. The temple prang is a cone tapering to the sky, a tower covered in thousands of seashells and pieces of colored porcelain. There is a row of clay warriors, their shinning eyes and armor made from tiny tiles. The spire seems to rest on their backs and arms. Circle the base clockwise, stopping to trace the ceramic flowers with your thumb. Imagine the hands that built these flowers turning to dust.

Look over the monastery from 150 feet. Watch the monks in orange robes glow against the grey footpaths and green shrubs. Somewhere monks are chanting. Their voices pour from horn loudspeakers posted throughout the complex. It's clearer at this height. It's a steady tone and rhythm, a stream of soft vowels. It's gapless. Their words are a river. You're swimming without water.

Had you noticed it before?

TAKE THE FERRY

The Chao Phraya runs along the east side of Wat Arun. There is a dock where you can catch a long-tail boat into the city. The dinghy rocks against the sturdy current. The breeze off the water smells like salt and iron and dirt. Breathe it in. On the approaching shore there is The Grand Palace spackled with flakes of gold, glittering.

Imagine the palace last night, covered in lights to commemorate Loi Krathong—a festival of letting go. Sky lanterns rise into the night like blooms of flying jellyfish. Thousands walk down to the river. Imagine you are caught in the wave of a new kind of intimacy. Together, under the Rama VIII Bridge, you light candles and make wishes and sail them downstream on flowery crowns of banana leaves and coconut husks. You notice a group of boys a few meters south, wading through the muddy water. They are fishing krathongs from the river, blowing out the candles and selling them to others waiting on the shore. Pray to the river goddess that your real hopes will continue to float.

HEAD EAST

Follow the floodwater lines running along the bottom of buildings. Sidestep garbage bags and puddles from dripping A/C window units above the street. The air is heavy, like a dank basement. Get lost in the buzzing of motorbikes and autorickshaws.

Take a right, now, onto an unnamed soi. It is too narrow for a car. The small road is lined with morning street-food vendors selling porridge and pastries, soup and dim sum.

Nod to people as you pass. Smile. They smile back.

TAKE THE SUBWAY AT HUA LAMPHONG

Walk around the front entrance to find an escalator leading down to a long tunnel, trapping the humidity from the city above. The walls are sweating. The high ceiling echoes a hundred sandals slapping the floor. The tunnel ends at a ticket counter. Purchase a fare to Thanon Sukhumvit and then take two more sets of escalators, down, down, to the Metropolitan Rapid Transit platform.

The train is arriving. A blast of cold air slaps your forehead as you push your way on. Pinned by a mass of people against the back wall of the passenger car, you can barely lift your arms. Unclench your fists. Slide a hand into your pocket and over your wallet. You can relax.

EXIT AT SUKHUMVIT (TERMINAL 21 MALL)

The stairs lead up from the subway to the ground-level entrance of a shopping complex designed like an airport terminal. The women at the info desk are dressed like flight attendants. The escalators are decorated like departure gates. Each floor is themed with a global city: Paris, Tokyo, London, Istanbul, San Francisco, and Hollywood. You are in Rome. There are pillars, arches, faux frescoes, and marble angels looking down on shoppers.

English is everywhere, and whether it is a spa promotion or a sale on high heels, for a moment you are literate again. You understand more than bits and pieces of passing conversations. Two young American men walk by wearing tank tops and folded bandana headbands. One of the boys has camouflage cargo pants, while the other has neon pink short shorts. They are having an argument over which street market is bigger, JJ or Chatuchak. Don't point out that JJ Market and Chatuchak Market are the same. Do not interject that many places in the city have more than one name in English, and the J sound and the Ch often get confused. Knowing makes you feel like less of a tourist.

HEAD WEST

At the bottom of the stairs exiting Terminal 21, there is a man with one arm and no legs lying on his belly. He shakes the change in his paper cup. The back of his T-shirt reads "I LOVE THE KING." Give him 20 baht, and then turn right.

Ignore the peddlers calling out to you. You may not know where you're headed or what you're looking for, but you know it is something larger than a trinket or souvenir. It is something less accessible than a watch, bong, or bootleg DVD.

Thanon Sukhumvit turns into Thanon Phloen Chit. There is construction everywhere. Crews of laborers in hardhats and flip-flops are raising new luxury condominiums from the rubble of old luxury condominiums. Above the chorus of jackhammers and drills are the staccato blasts of car horns. The exhaust fumes mix with the smell of street vendors grilling pork. Layers of black dust hug the street. It's harder to breathe. Somewhere people are chanting. It's coming from a gated square, ahead on the right.

ERAWAN SHRINE

The believers light incense and circle the shrine clockwise, laying wreaths of yellow flowers and bowing to the four faces of the Hindu god Brahma. Some are on their knees, their eyes squeezed tight in prayer. A few feet away, shielded from the sun by an open gazebo, a female dance troupe sways to a chorus of Thai folk songs. They wear towering headpieces and traditional dresses with shimmering layers that wrap around them and drape over their shoulders. Their faith makes them impervious to the heat.

Scan the crowded square for a depiction similar to the one at Wat Arun protruding from the temple prang—Indra, the lord of heaven, riding

Erawan, an elephant with three heads.

But there is no giant white elephant of the clouds. There is no Erawan at Erawan Shrine. Only Brahma.

Ask your spouse about this later, but don't get frustrated when she can't fully explain. She has spent the last decade living abroad. Much of what you will experience will also be new to her. The task of reacclimatizing to her old home means she may not always have time for your explorations. She has her own questions. You'll have to try to find your own answers. And you both may never find out why.

There may always be some facets of this city that elude your understanding, even its name. Is it Bangkok or Thonburi Si Mahasamut or Rattanakosin or Krungthepmahanakhon Amonrattanakosin Mahintharayutthaya Mahadilokphop Noppharatratchathaniburirom Udomratchaniwetmahasathan Amonphimanawatansathit Sakkathattiyawitsanukamprasit or just Krung Thep Maha Nakhon for short? Was the city named for its flowers or for its treasures gracing the ocean? The city of angels, great city of immortals, magnificent city of the nine gems, seat of the King, city of royal palaces, home of gods incarnate erected by Vishvakarman at Indra's behest.

Move closer. Follow the current circling the shrine. Press your palms together in respect for what you don't know.

DOGS IN THE KINGDOM

The narrow street smells like cooked rice and starched linens from the dry cleaner on the corner. It reeks of mildew, diesel, sewage, and cabbage boiled for too long.

Last night's unseasonal chill lingers under the overcast clouds and apartment building shadows. A rooster croons. A delivery truck brakes for a motorbike taxi carrying a girl in a grey pencil skirt. Her cinnamon thighs are folded over the side. With one hand she brushes her hair out of her face. The other hand grips her driver's reflective orange vest.

A grandmother in a stained cloth apron squats over a storm drain. She dumps brown water from a large steel bowl. Three dogs make slow circles around the old woman like satellites caught in the gravity of her hips. They wait for her to open her noodle soup stand. Every morning the old woman makes a plate of food and sets it on the curb for the local spirits. She lights incense and prays. The dog pack is fat from the offerings stolen from ghosts. The cracked pavement is littered with canine shit.

The dogs live in the rubble of a housing complex, a field of brick and sand and glass bordered by a cinderblock fence. The short wall runs parallel to the road for nearly fifty yards. A section of it has been destroyed, felled by time, roots, and floodwater.

A lone bitch is resting between the break in the wall. She is lean. Her short coat is the color of hay bales. A single streak of brown fur traces her spine to the tip of her tail. She watches the street. Her eyes ask: what are you?

She rises onto all fours. She trots closer.

Her ears drop. She does not bark.

She darts.

Her teeth sink through my slacks. There is a flash of hot burning like a match held close to the skin. My leg pulls forward out of her jaws. I kick her long snout. She backs away, growling. She spreads her legs and lowers the front of her body. Her eyes narrow to slits as she prepares to strike again. The both of us are unwilling to move. A few meters away a man springs from the driver seat of a parked car. He appears to have been waiting. He runs over waving his hands. He shouts, "No!" but not to the dog. "Go away, go!" he says, but not to the dog.

The bitch sits on her hind legs, staring at the man yelling wildly in her defense. Her head turns. Her gaze moves from my fists to my feet.

There is a squishing sound as my body turns to walk away. Warm blood trickles down my calf and dampens the sole of my right shoe.

~ ~ ~ ~

The nurse at Siriraj Hospital asks what happened.

I tell her a dog bit me.

"When?"

"This morning."

"Why didn't you come to hospital?"

I explain to her that I am enrolled in an intensive ESL teaching course. "It is accredited by the University of Cambridge. It's expensive. Literally, I can't afford to miss a day."

The nurse nods to say she understands but her eyes are concentrating on my mouth, the way my practice students do whenever I have lost them. My trainers say I have to learn to grade my language. Do not overwhelm them. Give only the information needed.

"I am a teacher," I say, and then in Thai, "Ajarn."

"It's good to get rabies shot in first twelve hours."

I look at my cellphone. "I still have half an hour."

I smile but the nurse doesn't.

It was one of my fellow trainees who convinced me to get a rabies shot. After sharing my story in the break room, she showed me a picture of a friend she had lost in South Africa. He had spent many years caring for abandoned animals. He had probably been bitten more times than he could count, but it was a nibble from a puppy that killed him. She said it had barely broken the skin.

This trainee went on to tell me about Thailand having the third highest rate of human rabies in the world behind India and Vietnam. Although a decade of awareness campaigns by the Ministry of Public Health and millions of dollars from the annual budget for post-exposure treatments had led to several of Thailand's provinces becoming rabies free, she said the prevalence of stray and feral dogs in Thailand is still a major challenge to rabies prevention.

Another trainee had spent part of his childhood in Mae Sot, a town northwest of Bangkok, on the border of Myanmar. He told me how most of the people in his neighborhood were reluctant to report free-ranging dogs, fearing that if the animal were euthanized, they would receive bad karma. He told me how some authorities refused to capture or destroy violent canines. If a street dog was suspected of being rabid, a brave or desperate soul might leave some poisoned meat where the animal slept. In another district, he had heard of a group of local men killing a dog that had been attacking children. They beat the dog to death with bats and heavy sticks. They did it together in order to divide the cosmic retribution. I thought of the man who came running to the defense of the dog that had attacked me. Around his skinny neck was a string necklace of Buddhist pendants, tiny depictions of sitting monks encased in plastic. They hung outside the collar of his sweat-stained polo shirt. They clicked and rattled as he shooed me away.

"Symptoms?" the nurse asks.

"I don't think so. I do feel itchy, especially around the bite."

I twist on the medical bed so she can see my leg. She bends down to look closer.

"I washed it once I got to work. I didn't have alcohol but I used soap and hand sanitizer."

"Why did the dog bite?"

"Why?"

"Yes." She repeats herself. "Why did the dog bite?"

"I don't know."

The nurse looks up at me, waiting.

"Maybe I am not good with dogs."

The nurse nods and stands straight. She says she is going to check my temperature and blood pressure. She explains that I will have to complete a vaccination course, five injections in the next month.

I swallow loudly and slide my fingers along the corners of the medical bed. The linens feel like paper. The nurse says not to worry. The hospital will give me a small booklet. It lists the dates I need to come in. I can carry it in my wallet. I tell her I am afraid of needles and finally she smiles. I ask her where on my body I have to receive the shots. In movies and television it's always the ass. She lifts my left sleeve and pokes the side of my arm with her finger, just below my shoulder. This gives me some relief.

The nurse tells me to wait. She pulls back the bone-white privacy curtain and disappears among the traffic of the open infirmary. I stay seated on the hard hospital mattress and scan the emergency ward for something familiar.

An elderly woman is perched on the edge of her medical bed. She is so small. Her khaki shorts and sleeveless shirt reveal patches of ripped skin on her left arm and leg. The wet wounds bleed from purple to red to pink to white. But she smiles, indifferent to her pain or in spite of it. She pulls her thin grey hair into a ponytail as she explains to a male orderly what happened. I can't speak Thai. I imagine she fell off a motorbike, perhaps trying to balance herself and the groceries. Perhaps an animal ran into the road and she crashed. Maybe she slid over jagged pavement to avoid hitting a dog.

I whisper to no one. "A dog."

A spark of anger is building to a bonfire. I think about what brought me here and what I said to the nurse.

Maybe I am not good with dogs?

I have enjoyed the company of many dogs but have never established a strong enough connection to identify myself as a dog person. When I was sixteen I spent a summer in Ghana with my father. Three dogs guarded my father's house. I bonded with the largest one, a gruff mutt my father had named Lassie. Lassie's short temper and aversion to anything new mirrored my own angst. At times, he seemed to feel as alien as I did. Lassie hated walks and the sun. He hated the hot, humid wet seasons and how they aggravated his asthma. He hated children and had nipped the fingers of kids curious enough to try to reach in past the gate to pet him. He was a fat dog with fur the color of dirty snow.

I tried all summer to teach him how to fetch. When I'd throw the ball he'd go after it but never bring it back. Lassie finally got it right the day I was leaving. He brought the ball back for the first and last time.

My father called me years later to tell me Lassie had died. He didn't say how and I didn't ask. I thanked him and hurried off the phone. However Lassie was killed, I am certain it was painful. There are a thousand ways for a dog to die, many of them cruel.

My mother had a brown pug named Simon Peter. She adopted him from a preacher. The solemnity of Simon Peter's name didn't fit his personality. Simon Peter was gregarious and playful. He would run to strangers and bark only if they refused to pet him. After college, I lived in my mother's house for six months and became partly responsible for Simon Peter. I started calling him Popo. I can't remember why.

Popo died two years after I moved out. He was in the yard on one of the hottest days of the summer. When my mother let him back inside, she noticed he was sluggish. He retreated to a room my mother had filled with stacks of shoeboxes and old clothes that had never been worn. On the phone my mother pleaded for me to come to the house right away to check on Popo, but I told her I was busy at work at city hall. I can't remember with what.

When I arrived, I found Popo lying under a sundress in a puddle of his own shit. He was breathing heavily and his wide pink tongue, caked with vomit, hung from the side of his mouth. I picked him up, wrapped him in a beach towel, and drove him to the nearest animal hospital. Simon "Popo" Peter died from heat exhaustion.

I paid to have him cremated.

I circled the house, scattering his ashes along a path he had worn into the grass.

For a long time my mother could not forgive herself. For a long time I couldn't forgive her either. When I was younger it was easier to shift blame. I tried not to think about what would have happened if I had gotten there sooner.

I debate whether or not to call my mother now. It is almost 6:00 p.m. here in the hospital, but it is too early in the United States. I decide to wait until after I've received my first shot. She will ask me what I am going to do. Eventually, I will have to leave the hospital. I will have to go home and the dog could be waiting.

I have to do something. Where can I find poison? Would antifreeze or a bar of chocolate work?

There is a pause in the chatter of the emergency ward. The pause rolls over the infirmary like a tsunami. In the absence of speech I am drowned in the hums and beeps of medical machines. I worry that this silence is somehow for me. The grey-haired woman with torn flesh is staring back at me like she can read my thoughts, like I have been thinking aloud, like she knows what I am considering.

She motions to the orderly. He guides her off the bed onto a footstool and down to the floor. She hooks her arm around his and he helps her limp away.

The chatter comes back louder than before. I sigh, relieved. The nurse returns to me.

"The King is leaving the building," she says. "We cannot give you the vaccination now."

I ask her to repeat it but I still don't understand.

"The King is on the other side of the building. Where the vaccination is."

"But I thought I needed to get my first injection in the first twelve hours."

She nods but says nothing. Her eyes are unapologetic. It can't be helped.

"How long before the King leaves?"

She shrugs.

I imagine tiny rabid dogs racing through my blood stream, chasing after white blood cells like rabbits and tearing them apart with sharp yellow teeth. I could die. The King would never know and neither would that dog. I hop down from the bed.

"Can I take a walk?"

The nurse looks confused.

"I need to use the bathroom."

She nods again and points towards a pair of large swinging doors at the end of the room.

I exit the infirmary and make a left. I pass the bathroom and continue along the wide corridor. My muscles are tight and my head aches. I'm thirsty but I don't want to stop for water. There is a chorus of murmurs under the squeaks of my shoes on the waxed floor. I look at the time on my phone. In less than a half of an hour I will surpass the preferred time for prevention.

How long before this kills me?

When do the seizures and foaming mouth start?

What will become of me, and what will become of that dog?

The cellphone screen lights up with a social media notification. When I first arrived at the hospital I had posted a Facebook status about being bitten. A lot of people I knew had shared similar experiences. "Happened to me in Thailand as well," one comment read. "Someone recommended I keep dog treats in my pockets. Don't try that. #itgetsworse." Browsing online I discovered dozens of visitor and expatriate forums about the street dogs of Thailand. Most of these cyber discussions mirrored what I had been told earlier in the trainee break room: This country is all about dogs; there are over a hundred thousand roaming Bangkok; there's a page about it on Wikipedia. Dog bites are the primary source by which rabies is transmitted in Southeast Asia and it is a common occurrence in Thailand.

I take no comfort in this event being a common occurrence. It doesn't make me feel better to know that I am not the first or the last person to have this happen. The thought of my death being averaged into a single line of health data only fuels my anger.

I must do something.

I consider the phone in my hand. My thumb scrolls over the glowing list of contacts. There is the name of my fellow trainee, the guy who knows about poisoning dogs. He will tell me where I could find a really strong rat poison. He might even have some. On my way home to my apartment I will buy some pork balls from the grandmother at the noodle soup stand. When the moment is right I will leave the poisoned meat by the gap in the brick wall. And if another dog eats it, it can't be helped. Those other dogs were probably in collusion with the dog that bit me. There could be a pack waiting for me when I leave the hospital. Sons of bitches. I will kill them all, every last dog. The wolves. I will set fire to their dens and murder their puppies.

My feet move decidedly forward, carrying me while my mind rages. A right at the end of the hall leads to an escalator. The revolving staircase rises to an expansive lobby with vaulted ceilings. Hundreds of patients and staff have gathered, kneeling, in long, curving rows. Among them I see the silver-haired woman from the infirmary. Her wounded legs are tucked beneath her.

The mass of bodies clears a pathway from the first floor elevators to the main entrance. The path is over twenty feet wide and no one appears willing to cross it. On the other side are the hospital pharmacy and my vaccine. I pace half the length of the man-moat before lowering myself onto the arm of a vacant loveseat.

The appearance of the King is preceded by a silence as vast and as deep as an ocean. All the air is sucked from the room by a collective gasp. In this vacuum everything is muted. Everything moves more slowly in reverence of this soundlessness. Waves ripple from the spokes of his hospital wheelchair. Heads bob, down and up again, as he passes. His face is softer than it is on calendars and money, and his shoulders have been rounded by the weight of the kingdom. But his eyes are the same eyes that stare down at me from movie screens and posters and giant billboards. They are strong and kind.

A leather strap tied to the right arm of the King's chair is fastened to the collar of the dog that bit me. Her blackened paws are now clean. Her once prominent ribs are hidden by new fat and fur. Her nose and eyes have changed, but I know it is her.

I wish for the dog to look over, to see me and to know that I recognize her, but her eyes are locked forward. She is ignorant of my wrath and the attention given to her master. She doesn't know or care that she is in the company of the King. She doesn't know his name, his long life of service, or all he has accomplished. She loves him for an entirely different reason, or for no reason at all.

And then I briefly imagine the crowd genuflecting not only to the majesty of His Highness the King but also in respect to the dog. They praise a devotion most humans are unwilling to give. They bow to that unswerving loyalty, that dogged love we can only aspire to, how it betrays a millennium of animal instinct, how it serves and provides us a deeper understanding of ourselves, and how it is in and of itself a kind of miracle.

The fury fades as I ponder whether or not dogs have a soul and what might happen to them when they die. I consider Buddhism, reincarnation, past and future lives. Maybe this isn't the dog from this morning. Maybe it could be. Maybe it is Lassie or Popo or one hundred thousand different dogs I will encounter while living in the capital of this kingdom.

My hand reaches into my front pocket. I turn off my cellphone. I rise from the arm of the loveseat and lower to my knees.

The King and his dog pass. They exit. Sound returns as people disperse to different parts of the hospital.

I rise again, calm, and return to the emergency ward.

LESSON PLAN

WEEK 1 (INTRODUCTIONS)

Course Title: *ENGLISH-IV (Academic Writing for Second-Language Learners)*
University Course Number: *BG2001*
Section: *434*

(0:00) / (1:30)

> Greet students as they enter.
>
> Don't officially start until ten after, to allow for late arrivals.

(0:10) / (1:30)

> Write your name on the board.
>
> Introduce yourself and welcome students to class.
>
> Pass around attendance sheet.

(0:15) / (1:30)

> Lead into icebreaker activity.
>
> Pair students and have them introduce their partners to the rest of the class.
>
> Encourage students to exchange contact information.

(0:50) / (1:30)

Distribute and discuss the syllabus.

Discuss classroom attendance policy and smartphone usage.

(1:10) / (1:30)

Place a chair at the front of the room below your name on the blackboard.

Take a seat and invite the class to ask whatever they are curious to know about you.

ANTICIPATED AND FREQUENTLY ASKED QUESTIONS

Can you rap?

—No.

Can you dance?

—Whenever I get the opportunity.

Can we touch your hair?

—I'd rather you didn't.

What do you like to eat?

—Food. Food is good.

Do you only teach?

—I'm a professional writer.

Do you have a Thai wife?

—I am married. She happens to be from here, Bangkok, and she is Thai.

Teacher, do you know Drake, Future, Chris Brown, 2 CHAINZ, LIL WAYNE, BIG SEANICKIMINAJUICYJAYZ!?!?!

—No. Not personally.

What about Will Smith or Tyrese?

—No.

Have you been to jail?

—Yes.

Were you in a gang?

—No.

Have you sold drugs?

—Yes, but that isn't why I was arrested.

Why were you arrested?

—I did something I shouldn't have done and it's a lot easier to get arrested in America when you look like me.

Why is it easier to get arrested?

—Because of racial bias, but it's a lot more complicated than that. Or maybe it isn't.

What is racial bias?

—Treating someone differently because of his or her skin color. Judging someone because of how they look.

Like Michael Brown or Eric Garner or Tamir Rice or Freddie Gray or Sandra Bland...or...or...?

—How do you know those names?

Social media hashtags.

—I see.

Is it like prejudice, when you think everyone is the same?

—Kind of.

But, teacher, we all are different, so why can't we treat each other differently?

—We are all different, and we are not the same, and yet we are. Does that make sense? I think all people should have certain inalienable rights.

What?

—Everybody should be respected and treated fairly. They should have the same opportunities.

Oh, okay...Do you hate white people?

—No.

Only white people can have racial bias?

—No.

Is racial bias only in America?

—Definitely not.

Is Thailand prejudiced?

EXAMPLES FOR CITATION

- The persecution of Thailand's hill tribes along the northern borders
- Blackface in Dunkin' Donuts advertisements in 2013
- The discrimination and political suppression experienced by Muslim Malays along the southern borders
- The ongoing mistreatment of Rohingya and other refugees
- The difficulty you and other dark-skinned people have experienced obtaining positions that are not labor intensive or geared towards the service industry
- The prevalence of white westerners in Thailand receiving better pay than people of color who have higher qualifications
- The abundance and popularity of skin-whitening creams, lotions, pills, and tonics
- The instance when a photography studio edited your work visa photos without permission, giving you lighter skin, a

thinner nose, and other Anglo-European features

Are we racist?

—You could be. So could I. But we should try not to be. I'm not sure how we do that, but I think asking questions helps, to ask and to listen.

Do you not like some of our questions?

—Some of your questions make me uncomfortable, but that is not always bad. My mother told me if you never ask, you'll never know.

Yes...Teacher, do you know Oprah or President Obama?

—No. Not personally.

Teacher, will you be a kind teacher?

—I'll try.

(1:25) / (1:30)

Before dismissing the class, assign pages from Unit 1 in the coursebook as homework.

Tell the students you look forward to learning with them.

FIGURES

Sometimes, when P and I walk holding hands in Bangkok, I will notice someone's confused gaze. "Just ignore it." I can't. "You know it's not like in America, in the South. Here they're staring because they don't understand. It's not hate." (Figure I) I glare at the observer, but they don't look away.

FIGURE I

Members of P's family have expressed their bewilderment.

Aunts and cousins have asked:

Why didn't she marry someone like her, Thai-Chinese?

Why, after spending over ten years in America, hadn't she chosen a white man instead?

With P already possessing coveted light eyes and hair, P's relatives believe her half-Caucasian children would have been beautiful. P's hypothetical offspring could have grown up to become Thai soap opera stars.

When I asked P how she felt about these comments, she offered me the same dismissive shrug I imagine she gives her inquisitive kin. On one occasion, P's indifferent gesticulation was mistaken for doubt, and a concerned cousin told P not to worry. The cousin said she understood—one can't help whom they fall in love with. She praised P's bravery. And, if P decided to have children, her cousin could procure supplements and traditional remedies to ensure the baby would not look black like its father.

P can repeat her cousin's words with a smile. "She means well. Try not to take it too personally."

I wonder how many other well-meaning people view my appearance as something in need of a remedy.

~ ~ ~ ~

The observer's eyes read over P and me, scanning for evidence to an omitted piece of data—the reason we came together. P has very fair skin and I am black, and this makes our union harder for the observer to understand.

If P had a tan complexion, the observer might find it easier to contextualize our association. They could assume we met in a go-go bar or a massage parlor. The observer would feel confident deducing P's origins from one of the impoverished provinces like Isan, where people are less inclined to carry umbrellas on cloudless days to avoid getting darker. With more melanin, P could fit into the popular Thai caricature of a poor brown woman eager to please a foreign man who can offer an alternative to a life of scarcity.

"Why do you care so much what people think? It doesn't matter."

But it does matter to me. (Figures II, III, and IV) The observer has defined most of my romantic relationships.

FIGURE II

My sophomore year as an undergrad, I started dating J. For nine months she spent most nights in my dorm room. She'd sneak over late and wake early to creep back to her own apartment.

For my birthday she bought me a five-inch retractable pocketknife, because she knew I often felt unsafe at the redneck roadhouses where she liked to sing karaoke renditions of her favorite Reba McEntire songs. We always made sure not to touch at these bars. We didn't want to incite the observer. In fact, J and I never showed any affection in public. We stayed mindful at all times of the proximity between us, so no one would have reason to suspect we dated.

J begged me to swear to secrecy. J feared her father might kill or disown her if he ever discovered her with a black boy.

Eventually, I started to resent her.

I began to provoke and test her.

I cheated on her with her friends.

J would scream about my behavior, but she never stopped tiptoeing to my bed each night.

At the end of the school year, my father came to visit me on campus. He brought my stepmother and my two half-sisters. I introduced them all to J. My father liked her. He appeared pleasantly surprised by J's appearance. He smiled broadly, chuckling at the idea of his African American son catching a white girl.

I never had a chance to meet anyone in J's family. We never had a talk about ending our relationship. I suppose we both knew I'd be unable to see or contact her over the summer while she stayed with her parents. We reconnected a few times the following fall, calling or texting each other whenever one of us felt lonely. We'd meet after dark in secluded locations. I'd drive to abandoned properties, quiet construction sites, empty playgrounds, and farm roads.

When I met P years later and we had a conversation about past partners, I didn't know if I should mention J. Like the conundrum of a tree falling in an uninhabited forest, if no one witnessed my time with J, did it ever really exist?

FIGURE III

After J, I became enamored of K.

K introduced me to several of her coworkers and family.

We met in an Etymology class.

We never dated officially.

She had a white boyfriend, but she said she was conflicted.

I wanted to be with K, but my feelings changed when I heard the ringtone she assigned to my number in her cellphone. Every time I called, her mobile erupted with the nasally refrain from The All-American Rejects' "Dirty Little Secret."

FIGURE IV

I started a long-distance relationship with M my senior year of college. We met for the first time when I went home to Maryland for Christmas.

M didn't express any internal conflicts about my race. She said she only dated black and brown men because she believed they all possessed larger penises and a better appreciation for her derrière. I told her these were stereotypes. "The good kind," she replied.

M felt the need to tell me whenever I did or said anything she considered white, because it made me less attractive to her.

I loathed most things M enjoyed and we had little in common.

A few weeks before we stopped speaking, M visited me in South Carolina. Unaccustomed to eliciting so many stares and furrowed brows, the attention excited her.

During her short stay, I took M to a popular shopping complex. While strolling aimlessly past the retail spaces, M pinched my sides to alert me whenever she perceived a disapproving glance. After the fifth sharp squeeze on my midsection, I asked M to consider the possibility the glares we received were in response to her penchant for public displays of affection, not my skin color. M shook her head. She explained to me how people still weren't fully ready to accept a relationship like ours—not everyone was as progressive as she was. M was certain no one would have scowled at us groping each other in front of a maternity clothes window display if we both were white. I didn't bother to argue with her. Her eyes narrowed mischievously. M leaned in to whisper in my ear. She said we should give the observer a better reason to scowl. We had sex in a handicapped stall in the women's restroom adjacent to the food court.

Contrary to her frequent and adamant condemnation of the observer, M never kissed me so hard as when she noticed someone watching.

I didn't care why M wanted me. I enjoyed feeling desired.

~ ~ ~ ~

The observer changes the nature of the subject; it is widely known one cannot measure the behavior of a system without affecting the system. The observer's curiosity prompts me to question my relationship with P. And this doesn't change with the observer's nationality or disposition. American or Thai, openly prejudiced or meaning well, the query behind their hypothesis remains the same: why would P choose a dark-skinned partner?

Every time I become aware of the observer, it compels me to search the relationship between P and me for missing variables to justify motivations. (Figure V) I sort through my own accounts for an explanation.

FIGURE V

The night of our wedding, P confessed to me how, at eleven or twelve years old, her mother took her to a fortuneteller. The soothsayer told P she would die in a plane crash, but not before marrying a large dark-skinned man who spoke a different language.

In middle school, the quirks I'd have as an adult became more apparent. My mother would joke about how I was destined to wed someone from another race. She'd say a black girl wouldn't have the patience to deal with me.

~ ~ ~ ~

How does what we are told influence whom we find attractive? "You think too much." Maybe. "Don't do what you usually do and start asking me questions about why I like you." Like? Not love? "I don't know what I need to say to prove it to you." There's no need to say anything. I have evidence. Living in Bangkok, I now have an even better appreciation of the concessions P was willing to make to stay with me. (Figure VI) "Then if you know how I really feel, shouldn't that be enough?"

FIGURE VI

Years earlier, in South Carolina, P's phone chimes between batches of thunder. I rise from the bed and slink through the dark. Lighting breaks through the slits of the venetian blinds and for a few seconds I can see P stirring under a pile of comforters. I move across the room towards her cellphone perched on the corner of the dresser. When the light fades the neon fluorescent glow of the dial pad burns through the black. I grab the phone and retreat back to bed.

P rises onto her elbows with a groan. I tap a key to accept and hand her the phone. She coughs to clear her throat. She answers in Thai. Her salutation sounds apprehensive.

She worries one day she will receive a call that will ask her to find money we don't have and travel to the other end of the Earth for a family emergency.

I worry about this too.

I lie down next to P and press my hand firmly against her back. I ready myself to pull her into a hug if the call relays tragedy. I wait, listening for inflections of sadness and tapping my foot impatiently against nothing.

After a few minutes, she pulls the phone from her ear and her face vanishes into the darkness. She sighs and tells me her family is okay and her father is planning to retire.

I exhale, unaware that I had been holding my breath.

She nestles into my arms, and I ask why she chose me when it means living so far away from her home and everyone she loves. She grunts, "Whatever, Donald."

And although P can't offer me a definitive answer, in her tone and in her actions I sense that even when The Call comes P won't regret having decided on me.

Despite the storm roaring outside, I return soundly to sleep.

~ ~ ~ ~

I first got to know P in South Beach, Miami during a spring break trip sponsored by our college's international student organization. P and I discovered that we shared a lot of similar interests and ideals, and we quickly became friends. In Miami, P saw me fight with M on the phone several times. P watched me text and rendezvous with K, who also happened to be in South Beach with some friends. And, after finding out K's boyfriend had accompanied her to Florida, P witnessed me drink until I passed out in the doorway of my room at the Starlite Hotel.

As friends, P never offered her thoughts on my behavior or my interactions with other women, even though I often asked for her perspective. When we began dating, P refused to remark on my prior relationships. Even now she shows no interest in sorting through my past, always urging me forward.

"Hey, forget it. Let's keep going, Donald." She reminds me not to allow the judgment of others to shape my perception of us. Regardless of whether someone else understands what they see when they look at us, we do not owe anyone an explanation for our attraction. With P I know I am loved, not fetishized. I am not taboo.

I'LL FLY AWAY:
NOTES ON ECONOMY
CLASS CITIZENSHIP

UNITED AIRLINES (NRT > BKK) NOVEMBER 2012

I fly to Southeast Asia to begin living in Thailand, a country I have briefly visited twice. Many factors contribute to my decision to leave the United States, but whenever asked I only provide one: "Because I want to focus on writing."

During a connecting flight from Narita International Airport to Suvarnabhumi, I read *The Cross of Redemption*, an anthology of previously uncollected writings by James Baldwin. One of my sisters from my father's second marriage gave me the book as an early birthday/Christmas/parting gift. In one of Baldwin's essays, "On Language, Race, and the Black Writer," a passage shakes my bones:

> ...for a black writer in this country to be born into the English language is to realize that the assumptions on which the language operates are his enemy. For example, when Othello accuses Desdemona, he says that he "threw a pearl away rich-

er than all his tribe." I was very young when I read that and I wondered, "Richer than his tribe?" I was forced to reconsider similes: "as black as sin," "as black as night," "blackhearted."

In order to deal with that reality at a certain time in my life, I left the United States and went to France, where I was unable to speak to anybody because I spoke no French. I dropped into a silence in which I heard, for the first time, the beat of the language of the people who had produced me. For the first time, I was able to hear that music.[1]

Thirty-two thousand feet above Vietnam, lost in this essay, Baldwin articulates my desire to live abroad. I want to drop into silence.

I am moving to Thailand because I want to focus on writing, yes, and I want to escape from the everyday oppression I feel as a person of color in America. I want to break from a continued and systematic white supremacy so pervasive it is entrenched in the vernacular I use to express myself.

I have never felt nationalistic, and I have an aversion to most things identified as intrinsically American, especially literature. In school, I had to read *Adventures of Huckleberry Finn* because I'm American and it is a great American novel. I remember Twain's work never really spoke to me, and like Baldwin, I found it hard to identify with the "ethical dilemma" concerning Nigger Jim. As Baldwin explains in his aforementioned essay, "It was not, after all, a question about whether I should be sold back into slavery."[2]

Many experiences in America confirm what I've always felt. A majority of the slave-owning founding fathers did not consider someone like me when they scrawled "all men are created equal" onto that famous parchment. In America, I spend a lot of time fighting about my unalienable rights. A lot of my focus goes into having to explain my civil liberties.

1   James Baldwin and Randall Kenan, *The Cross of Redemption: Uncollected Writings* (New York: Pantheon, 2010), 114.

2   James Baldwin and Randall Kenan, *The Cross of Redemption*, 114.

As my flight lands at BKK, I consider a question Baldwin heard Malcolm X ask a young sit-in student: "If you are a citizen, why do you have to fight for your civil rights? If you are fighting for your civil rights, then that means you are not a citizen."[3]

Can one feel a sense of citizenship in a place they've been made to fear? Some parents teach their children to respect authority; my mother taught me to be invisible. At a very young age she told me the law protects some men and victimizes others. She encouraged me to stay vigilant and to avoid situations that might bring me in contact with law enforcement. She told me, when confronted by a cop—not if, when—keep quiet; be apologetic; don't talk back. "They don't need a reason to arrest you," she said. "They will kill you."

I know many honorable men and women serving as police officers. However, when I see the badge and uniform, I often have difficulty forgetting my mother's warning and the many instances where her words felt true. I find it difficult to forget my first safety belt violation, because the officer's hand never left the grip of his gun as he spoke; his pointer finger floated between the barrel and the trigger guard. I didn't dare correct him. Before he excused me I found the courage to look down at the polyester strap hugging my chest to make sure I hadn't imagined putting it on. I understood then that it didn't matter if I believed I was wearing my seatbelt. The officer was the law. The officer taught me a frightening lesson, something my mother had tried to explain. He didn't need reason. Racism in America includes the ability to ignore what should be seen; it thrives on a system in which one group's perception is considered more factual than another. The officer tilted his head. Staring at the restraint stretched across me, he told me to have a good day.

I remember being seventeen. On a fall evening, leaned against the rear hatch window of my mother's Ford Explorer parked a few feet from my front door, I was talking with two friends, one black the other Latino. A police cruiser rolled up. An officer stepped out and asked for ID. While he crosschecked our names with his dashboard computer, he instructed us to lie facedown in the street with our bellies and palms pressed against the

3   James Baldwin and Randall Kenan, *The Cross of Redemption*, 115.

cold, wet asphalt. I stayed quiet, but one of my friends spoke up from the ground, shouting at the officer: "He lives right there. You see his address on the driver's license, right? That's his house. We're from this neighborhood. We're the good teenagers."

Once the officer was done, he ordered us to rise. He returned our identification and told us not to stand around because it makes people nervous. "You shouldn't be here," he said.

The officer's words lingered long after I had finished shaking the damp leaves from my clothes. I have never stopped debating if he was right. Tucking Baldwin's collection into my backpack, I head to the baggage claim wondering if it was ever possible to belong to a place where I am expected to vanish to avoid being erased.

NIPPON AIRWAYS (SEA > NRT) MARCH 2014

What has to be unseen, kept visible, to make you dead to a culture? The clothing, the language? The color of the hair or eyes? Can you move to a city? Can five pots save you? Sixteen drops of blood? Yes, the blood, kept in a little sanctified vial. In the end, how scientific is this vision of race and life: that existence depends on objects that are quantified, preserved, capitalized upon. The human body on its own isn't enough to prove a life, let alone a way of it.[4]

At the AWP conference in Seattle, I attended a panel where Paisley Rekdal spoke about her memoir, *Intimate: An American Family Photo Album*, and how it incorporates prose, poetry, creative nonfiction, and photography to examine cultural identity.

---

4   Paisley Rekdal, *Intimate: An American Family Photo Album* (North Adams, MA: Tupelo, 2011), 158.

I am finishing Rekdal's book somewhere far above the Pacific Ocean on a flight back to Bangkok, and it leads me to consider how we define race and what parameters we use to determine who belongs to a population.

What makes me African American?

What makes me black?

My language? My skin? My hair? My experiences?

What is an Oreo or a house nigger or an Uncle Tom? I've been called these things for as long as I can remember. Whatever it means to be black, why am I not black enough for some and too black for others?

I remember every instance a person has characterized me as a traitor to my race.

I remember friends of all colors teasing about how white I am, citing the way I speak, the shows I watch, the music I listen to, and what I read as evidence of my unbearable whiteness.

I rise from my seat to stretch by an emergency exit door. Members of a Thai tour group watch me bend, pull, and bow. I smile, and they smile back.

I wonder how they view me. To them I am black. Is that all they see?

My skin tone is not desirable to many Thais. Darker skin complexions are common among laborers and the perception is that those who work in the sun have less money. Neocolonization and popular Western media that propagate Anglo standards of beauty reinforce these perceptions about skin color and class. There are prejudices, but in spite of the apparent hierarchy associated with skin color, I am profiled less in Bangkok. Fewer expectations and presumptions are based on my race.

I remember that at my previous job I was once late for an offsite meeting with two white coworkers. After I arrived they made jokes about how, if they were racist, they could say I suffered from colored-people time.

I remember how I used to eat fried chicken in restaurants until one day when deciding where to have lunch with a black schoolmate I suggested a wings place. She sighed and said, "You really want to perpetuate that stereotype?"

In Thailand I don't have to worry about how my actions will speak for others or how my choices play into narratives forced upon me. Most Thai citizens are unfamiliar with any African American stereotypes I may affirm or dispel. I can't imagine a Thai person calling me a nigger or an Oreo. They see I am black, but the white gaze does not pock my skin. My blackness is not determined by what it is not.

Leaving America provided me an opportunity to see myself in different social constructs. I am free to invent myself, unburdened by America's history of aggression towards black bodies. I can build my own narrative.

I think of Rekdal as I return to my row, side-stepping to avoid a flight attendant distributing tiny cups of water. "THREE SUBJECTS circling each other," Rekdal writes. "Eros, identity, and elegy. A natural progression. In love with the newest mask, we strip each covering back to another version of the self."[5]

Is this new freedom I enjoy in Thailand the result of donning a new mask, or do I feel more freedom because I've removed the guises I wore to survive America?

CHINA AIRLINES (ATL > AMS > BKK) JUNE 2015

Does the altitude prompt me to think about how race and identity are irrefutably chained to citizenship? The constant roar of the jet turbines and the sound of air rushing past become a long hymn conducive to reflection. On eighteen-hour flights I rise out of time and cross a dozen borders. I don't inhabit a continent. I am removed. In transition between destinations and identities, I find it easier to think about nationality, perhaps more objectively. I have no affiliations in the sky. It's only me and a few hundred others. A small nation of travelers soaring miles above earth and sea. Up here there exist apparent hierarchies too. Some receive preferred treatment; they have

5   Paisley Rekdal, *Intimate*, 236.

advantages because of the position of their seat and row. I don't know why it has to be the same on the ground or why some are expected to accept economy class citizenship.

I am thinking all this on the first flight of my return trip to Bangkok, from Atlanta to Amsterdam. I was in South Carolina visiting friends and family. In Greenville, South Carolina, I found a copy of Claudia Rankine's *Citizen: An American Lyric*. I read it once, and I read it again on the connecting flight from the Netherlands to Thailand.

The book makes me angry. I am infuriated by my familiarity with the experiences described. Rankine captures the exasperation of being a black American in the twenty-first century. She examines a frenzy that comes from being told to calm down while a nation tries to devour you.

> Everything shaded everything darkened everything shadowed / is the stripped is the struck— / is the trace / is the aftertaste. / I they he she we you were too concluded yesterday to know whatever was done could also be done, was also done, was never done— / The worst injury is feeling you don't belong so much / to you—[6]

Rankine explains the origins of the same maddening frustration that led to violent clashes in areas of Missouri following the killing of Michael Brown. The same ire witnessed in the unrest in my home state of Maryland after the murder of Freddie Gray.

I remember watching news coverage of rioters tearing through Ferguson and Baltimore. I recognized that fury. I understood the rage born from feeling ignored for so long, let down for so long, the feeling that I don't really own anything but a life and body consistently threated by a governing structure that promises to protect me. I recognized the desire to burn it all down in hopes of rising from the ashes.

---

6   Claudia Rankine, *Citizen: An American Lyric* (Minneapolis: Graywolf, 2014), 146.

I often ask myself in flight, "Am I a citizen?" I mean more than legally.

During dinner with some friends in America, someone at the table asked me when I planned to return to the States to live. I told them I wasn't sure I would return, and I wasn't sure I'd want to. Another friend at the table asked me to explain, and I told them, "In Thailand I can get a sense of what it must feel like to be white in America, and it's nice." We all laughed nervously.

I've never been white in America but I assume it means the freedom to go where one wants without having to prepare an explanation. I imagine being white in America includes having the freedom to arrive late without it being indicative of an entire race, and having the ability to talk outside with friends in one's own neighborhood without being viewed as suspicious. These things are commonly associated with white privilege and I have only ever experienced them living in Thailand. I have a sense of freedom that I never had at home.

I was talking with a Thai friend who spent his childhood in the same area of Maryland where I grew up. We discussed the shooting of Walter Scott in North Charleston. He asked if I watched the cellphone video, and I nodded. He asked if I planned to visit America during the summer and I told him yes.

"Are you sure you want to do that?" he asked. "It's crazy over there. Is it even safe for you to drive around?"

"You know," I said, "it's always been like this, right?"

"Sure," he said, "but now I know about it, and you know you can be somewhere else."

If I am a citizen of the United States, why did I have to move to the other side of the world to escape the anxiety, resentment, frustration, and danger inherent to living as a black man in America? And why am I accused of race-baiting when I try to pose these questions or share my experience? If I am told to forget all I remember, isn't that an attack on my citizenship?

The plane begins the long descent and I ponder World War II and its role in the foundation of the African American Civil Rights Movement. While serving throughout Europe and the South Pacific, black soldiers experienced freedoms they did not have in the country of their birth. I can't relate to fighting for a country that doesn't fight for me. But now I can better imagine black soldiers like Medgar Evers returning to the United States and seeing how far away they were from equal. It is discouraging that sixty years after the start of the movement so many promises are still unfulfilled, and I'm urged to use hashtags to remind fellow citizens that my life matters.

A nation which aspires to noble ideas—life, liberty, and the pursuit of happiness for all—must first acknowledge how it falls short of those governing principles. A country that congratulates itself on being a global liberator should make the emancipation of populations within its own borders a priority. The United States must first acknowledge that some have more freedom than others and then examine why this is allowed to continue. This can't be done when those subjugated by America are silenced or dismissed. When citizens would rather ignore systems of oppression than admit how they might profit from them, when citizens victimized by those same oppressive institutions are told to get over it because their voice makes others uncomfortable, America fails.

DISEMBARKATION

When the plane lands in Bangkok I will sleep for days and awake to headlines of a church shooting in Charleston. I will recall over a dozen attacks on predominantly black houses of worship in South Carolina since the 1970s. I will remember six lives claimed by a similar evil at a Sikh temple in Oak Creek, Wisconsin in 2012. I will think of the 16th Street Baptist Church bombing in Birmingham, Alabama in September of 1963.

I'll be reminded of a page in Rankine's *Citizen* that lists recent black casualties to systemic racism, and in the blank spaces that follow the names Walter Scott and Freddie Gray, the book should be updated to include, "In Memory of Cynthia Hurd, Susie Jackson, Ethel Lance, Rev. De-Payne Middleton-Doctor, the Honorable Rev. Clementa Pinckney, Tywanza Sanders, Rev. Daniel Simmons Sr., Rev. Sharonda Coleman-Singleton, and Myra Thompson."

I'll watch outrage shift as social media explodes with impassioned status updates by white friends demanding legislators remove the confederate flag from statehouses. And I will wonder if these allies believe that they can throw racism away with Dixie Outfitters apparel. I won't like or leave a comment because I'll have noticed the sales of confederate flags on Amazon.com rose sharply before the company decided to remove them from stock, and because removing the confederate flag from plain sight makes it harder for me to identify those nostalgic for an era in America when blacks couldn't have citizenship. I'll keep quiet because symbolic gestures often have been used to avoid the real work of bridging gaps between disparities, and I'm not sure how sending the flag underground will advance the lives of a population forced behind.

Rebel colors will come down across the country with a wave of new arsons and bomb threats on black religious institutions. I will be incensed. Before anger eats me alive I can close my laptop. I can turn off my phone. I can take a walk, get lost in a crowded part of Bangkok, and not have to worry about being noticed. I can run my fingers over the embossed cover of my passport and consider the guilt and privilege I feel to be able to fly away.

JUNIOR

Thinking about you, I nearly collide with a Buddhist monk as I exit a Starbucks. I mime an apology to the robed gentleman. He pauses from chatting on his flip phone to smile at me, no harm done.

I don't notice the soy cappuccino dribble on my hand until I've joined a line for the taxi queue outside the shopping mall. The humidity makes it difficult to feel the sticky beverage on my damp skin.

I chug the remainder of my drink. With a napkin I grabbed from the coffee shop, I wipe my fingers. I don't see a recycling bin nearby, so I fold the receptacle and tuck it into an empty pocket in my messenger bag to dispose of later.

I check my watch. The Immigration Bureau offices reopen from their lunch break soon. A police officer waves me up to the next pink Toyota Corolla. I climb into the back seat. I shut the door. The meter beeps and we start moving.

Before the military took control of the country I had more difficulty getting taxis in Thailand because of my complexion. Since the National Council for Peace and Order mandated that all drivers dress better and accept all passengers, I can always walk to the nearest Skytrain or Metropolitan Rapid Transit station. At these locations a cop usually waits beside the line of potential fares, ready to issue a fine to any cabbie that refuses to accept a customer.

I tell the driver my destination. I hear "okay" in Thai, but the sigh that follows says the distance will inconvenience him. I scan the cab. A collection of clacking plastic religious pendants dangles from the rearview mirror. Below the holy jewelries is a turtle bobble-figure glued to the dashboard. A three-spoke racing wheel that you might see in the *Fast and Furious* films replaces the factory steering. Above our heads, a Theravada blessing scrawled in white clay paste punctuated with flecks of gold paper offers protection on our journey together.

On the bottom corner of my window, small yellow vinyl decals clarify the driver's rules: a cigarette, a beer bottle, and a hamburger, each in its own circle covered by a forward slash. A fourth sticker features a silhouette of a naked woman. She also has a circle around her, but the letters OK replace the strikethrough.

I don't remember ever seeing symbols like these in your taxi.

~ ~ ~ ~

All my life you have made money driving a taxi around Washington, D.C. You wake up each day after the early morning rush hour of the Beltway. You ride into the capital from Maryland; you might stop for lunch or coffee if you haven't packed food and a thermos. You drive late into the evening, arriving home long after dark.

I've always admired your work. As a child, being a taxi driver seemed to me a lot more interesting than confinement to a desk cubicle like my mother. Although your job has routine, you face constant deviations and obstacles you must circumnavigate: street closures for road accidents, presidential motorcades, demonstrators, shootings, and terrorist threats. You have freedom to make your own schedule. You get to explore and meet new people. One time, you took Darryl McDaniels of Run-D.M.C. to the airport and he gave you a tour sweatshirt.

Another time a person tried to rob you at gunpoint. You grabbed the pistol and kicked the mugger. You took the weapon, but when the assailant turned to flee you chased him down the block.

Mom likes to tell the story of how—while you both still lived together—I once chased after you. We must have just finished playing in the front yard. Although a toddler, I managed to unlock the gate to follow your taillights as you headed to work. A kind stranger reunited me with my mother later the same day. I was discovered a quarter mile from home and rescued before I tried to cross Montgomery Village Avenue.

In the third grade I asked you if I could spend the day riding in your cab. You seemed excited about the idea. We didn't get to see much of each other, even though I went to your place every day after school. At your apartment I spent most of my time with your wife and my half-sisters. When Mom finished work in the evenings, she would come to take me home with her. I usually left before you returned. We both recognized a day together as a much needed opportunity to reconnect.

Unfortunately, I got motion sickness trying to read a book while the car rocked like a boat in the stop-and-go traffic. By the early afternoon I knelt on the floorboard with my head rested on the front passenger seat, trying to dam the waves of nausea crashing in my gut. I pleaded for you to take me home. I never asked to ride with you again, and you never offered.

I had dreamed of growing up to have a career as an author and a taxi driver. But I didn't appear suited for the latter. I cried that night in bed beside my mother. She asked me what was wrong but I didn't know how to tell her the outing had forced me to acknowledge the growing divide between you and me.

You and I have always exhibited notable differences in personality, and for more than half my life I have weighed more than you. But I yearned to possess at least one trait indicative of you, if not physically then mentally.

~ ~ ~ ~

I reach into the front left pocket of my pants and remove my phone. I search through the saved images until I find a picture of you. You stand in knee-high rubber boots in front of a chicken-wire fence. Behind you a group of hens wander and peck aimlessly. Your jean shirt, soiled with perspiration and dirt, sags off your shoulders. Under your prescription sunglasses I can still see your tired eyes, but your hands rest proudly on your waist and I notice the small smirk below your greying beard.

The snapshot comes from the Mangoase farmland you and I bought together with some of the money my wife and I earned selling our restaurant before moving to Thailand. I had intended to use some of the land to launch a food cooperative with farmers in the region, but it proved hard to conceive while living between Thailand and the USA.

Now it has become your retirement plan. A project that might validate the years you toiled. The farm could give meaning to the mistakes you've made, the moments you've missed, the hurt you've caused, and the pain you carry on your back. Over the years you've increased the trips to Ghana and extended the duration of your stays to ensure that the farm's harvests succeed.

In my adolescence I resented your ties to West Africa and your jaunts abroad. I cursed the Gold Coast whenever you couldn't attend a school event because you were too busy trying to earn money to send overseas, or whenever I eavesdropped on your phone calls with my mother and you'd tell her you couldn't help financially because you had to save for pilgrimages to Africa. Every summer you vanished to Ghana with a trash bag full of my old clothes and toys. I'd seethe at the thought of you distributing my garments and action figures to other children. I'd picture you in Accra buying expensive rounds of Guinness and Heineken for your old schoolmates while my stepmother and sisters shared canned meat and disposable cups of instant noodles.

By the end of middle school I had grown too big to whip with a belt. Recognizing my salient disdain for Ghana, you threatened to send me to live with my grandmother in Teshie whenever my mother or stepmother reported to you that I had misbehaved.

I nearly repeated the eighth grade due to my violent conduct. You had to collect me from the principal's office on two occasions, including a time when I had been caught fighting another student for stealing and reading my poetry aloud on the bus to school. I remember that day well because you said my bulk, compounded by my tender demeanor and affection for trench coats and berets would only continue to goad the other black kids into harassing me.

You had to pick me up from school again a few months later for assaulting a fellow student in the cafeteria during lunch. I had returned to classes that day after serving a two-week suspension. Yomi, a Nigerian boy who also lived in your apartment complex, had demanded the chocolate milk from my school lunch tray. He hoped to assimilate himself with some of my usual tormentors, the same kids that teased him for his dark skin and accent. They called him Kunta and FOB (fresh off the boat). Sometimes they'd chant, "Yomi ain't no homie!" When I refused, Yomi snatched the dairy carton and laughed loudly. I shoved my hand into his open mouth and hooked his front teeth with three of my fingers. I pulled him to the floor and managed to drag him several inches before he thought to bite my knuckles. I yelped in pain and a school resource officer ran over to separate us. The assistant principal told you she planned to petition to have me expelled from the school district.

In your taxi, I pressed myself hard against the passenger side door. I clenched tightly, awaiting your fists and slaps. I knew you couldn't reprimand me for fighting because it was one of the few things about me that you could comprehend; you believed a man shouldn't allow himself to be bullied or intimidated. Instead, you shouted about the inconvenience, how you should have been driving at that moment, how you were losing fares, money you needed to take care of responsibilities in Ghana. We arrived at your building. Once we entered the apartment and the door locked behind you, you gripped my face. I returned your glare and you slapped me. Pushing me hard against a wall, you pinned my chest with your forearm and said, "I borne you."

You surprised me that night by calling my mother's townhouse and asking her to give you custody over me. My mother agreed, conceding that I could use discipline. I announced myself on the telephone line. I had been eavesdropping on another handset.

I refused to live with you. You ignored me. You yelled at my mother and issued her an ultimatum. If she didn't bring me to you that night, I would never be welcomed in your home again. I shrieked for you to apologize. I warned that if you didn't say sorry to Mom, I would kill you. You both fell silent, your voices replaced in my ear by the sound of my own heavy breathing. I said, "I hate you," and slammed the receiver to the hook.

I thundered out of the house.

I spent the night curled on a bed of cold, wet pine needles beneath a line of shrubs outside a Methodist church on Montgomery Village Avenue.

~ ~ ~ ~

Thinking about that evening conjures a fresh swell of embarrassment. I raise my glasses and pinch the bridge of my nose. I regret what I said and did. I can recognize your intentions now; you meant well. You asked to bring us closer and I ran away. I sigh and lean forward. The sweat down my spine has seeped through my shirt and adhered me to the pleather cushions of the cab's back seat. I roll my neck, reach a hand behind me, and peel the fabrics apart. I pull my shirt from my body and it makes a gentle sucking sound.

I've never apologized, but I assume you forgave me. I stayed with my mother, and the next year I started high school in a new district. I saw you even less. You must have noticed. The summer before my senior year, you told me you wanted to take a family trip to Ghana and asked if I would like to join. I said yes, happy for the chance to see my paternal grandmother again and spend time with my stepmother and sisters.

That summer I learned that your obligations did extend across the ocean. Your modest career as a taxi driver in America provided your wealth in Ghana, and you used your economic status to help others. Over eight weeks I observed you open the gates of your impressive villa to grant a few microloans, cover education fees and provide school supplies for children, allow local access to the clean drinking water in your well, and throw a party feeding your extended family. I finally grasped the depths of your kindness and generosity, and acknowledged that although you may not have been a great father or husband, you try to be a good man.

While together in Ghana, you volunteered to teach me how to drive a manual transmission. This culminated in me crashing your pickup truck into a street gutter, snapping the front axle and one of your ring fingers on the dashboard. I pressed myself hard against the driver side door and clenched tightly, awaiting your wrath, but you calmly instructed me to climb out of the vehicle. We walked away from the accident and marched quickly on the red clay road back to your property. Dozens of smiling eyes peeked at us from cinderblock huts and the convenience shops housed in old shipping containers. I thought I heard folks laughing until I realized that the soft chuckles belonged to you between winces of pain.

That summer I lost some fat and gained muscle. Before I came with you to Ghana, I had attended a single practice for my high school's football team on a whim and intended to join the varsity players in the fall. You greatly approved of this and said playing sports would make sense of my size. You further supported the endeavor by giving me a few cedis to get a membership at a nearby gym, and you made sure my grandmother controlled my food portions at every meal.

When I returned to school, I joined the marching band instead. You stuttered and screamed over the phone when I told you. Between expletives you said you didn't understand why I made life so hard for myself. You demanded to know why I would rather "parade around the football field with a sousaphone like a fat faggot." And I considered lying and telling you I was gay to make you choke on your own disappointment.

~ ~ ~ ~

I glance away from my phone. The road looks unfamiliar. I search outside my window for a landmark I might recognize, but I don't find anything that tells me this will lead to my destination. The taxi sputters climbing a bridge over a brackish waterway littered with foam containers and plastic bottles. Along the railings of the bridge, men cast fishing lines into the murky channel. In the distance, lurking over a row of copper shanties, a sun-scorched billboard displays a message from the junta: "We Promise to Restore Peace and Order and True Democracy to the People of Thailand."

Did you see similar signage growing up in Ghana under the shadow of the National Liberation Council and the National Redemption Council and the Supreme Military Council?

As a boy, you witnessed Ghana's first freely elected black government overthrown by a US-supported coup d'état in February 1966. I've asked you about those events but you've never offered any significant details. Once, walking together through the Kwame Nkrumah Mausoleum in Accra, we saw two black and white photographs in the adjoining museum. In one image, President Kwame Nkrumah converses with JFK. In the other, Nkrumah shakes hands with Chairman Mao. You leaned over to whisper to me, "They made the coup to kick him out because they feared he'd go communist."

In college, I read President Nkrumah's book, *Dark Days in Ghana*, to learn more about my heritage and know more about you. Written during his exile in Guinea, Nkrumah examines how foreign pressure and neo-colonialist interests spurred the destabilization of Ghana and other newly independent African states in order to usher in a new kind of economic imperialism. As you suggested during our museum visit, Nkrumah asserts that his foreign policy of non-alignment steered Western leaders to believe Ghana required regime change. He speaks about how the American media encouraged public support for the US military and CIA intervention that delayed his nation's total liberation.

I wonder how you consolidate these two identities: African and American.

Nkrumah's account frustrates me, because I know its truth. As an African American, I'm acutely aware of how my country uses various forms of media to propagate and justify attacks on people of color.

The first dog-eared page in my worn copy of *Dark Days in Ghana* features a letter to Kwame Nkrumah from the American expatriate Richard Wright, author of *Native Son*. In the haunting note—written six years before Wright's death and twelve years before Nkrumah's ousting—Wright warns of colonialist threats to Ghana's emancipation. "Make no mistake, Kwame," he says, "they are going to come at you with words about democracy; you are going to be pinned to the wall and warned about decency; plump-faced men will mumble academic phrases about 'sound' development; gentlemen of the cloth will speak unctuously of values and standards..."[7]

Wright's predictions refer to a lengthy history of oppression: the tendency of the United States to actively repress populations longing to free themselves from servitude and subservience, and its propensity to construct narratives to validate those intrusions on bodies of color. This predisposition is woven into the fabric of America's identity and has shaped much of America's foreign policy since World War II.

Acknowledging the role your adopted country played in destabilizing your home, there has to exist an internal conflict.

I wanted to ask you about this a few years ago, the last time we saw each other in person. I had flown to America to attend my MFA graduation in Vermont. I told you and the rest of the family not to bother coming to the ceremony, but I decided to spend a night visiting with you and my stepmother before leaving the country again. You came home late from driving your cab all day to find me on the floor of my sister's childhood bedroom, packing a suitcase for my return flight the following morning.

You said I looked slimmer and surmised the move to Thailand had been good for P and me.

You asked if I was okay.

I wanted to tell you about how leaving makes me feel like a traitor, and about how it feels whenever I read news about black suffering in America. I meant to ask you if the advantages of living in a place ever make it easier to forgive its crimes. I wished to voice to you the conflict I experience daily while enjoying the benefits I have in Thailand and the knowledge that so many are silenced and detained by the same governing force that has made it easier for me to hail a cab. I wanted to discuss military dictatorships promising democracy, decency, values, and standards while violating civil liber-

---

7   Kwame Nkrumah, *Dark Days in Ghana* (New York: International, 1968).

ties, and talk about how every day I witness others bear the type of suppression that led you to emigrate from Ghana.

If I were bolder when we last met, I would have asked if you could forgive me for absconding to a country notorious for the kind of political instability and despotism you hoped your children would never have to endure.

In response to your question I only managed to mention the guilt of living so far away from my ailing mother.

"Sometimes I feel selfish," I said, because I knew you'd understand, because now when I look in the mirror I often see the same rubbed-red, jet-lagged eyes and solemn expression that you bore the year your mother died on the other side of the Atlantic.

You laughed like I've seen you do when reminiscing with friends who shared your journey to America, and you told me I have to do what's best for me and go wherever I find opportunity to live better.

~ ~ ~ ~

The taxi parks at the mouth of a tight, dark alleyway lined with canopied food stalls. I don't recognize the location, but the driver tells me I've come to the correct place. He waves me out.

I don't argue. I pay him and step onto the grimy street. The taxi speeds off to the next fare and I am stranded on a busy city block I don't know. Unsure what to do, I amble forward.

Maybe my destination lies on the other side of the slender thoroughfare.

I waddle through the crowds packed between the food vendors, and I emerge from the alley with curry shrimp paste and warm cooking oil smoked into my flesh. A ferry waits at the end of a floating dock. The vast, brown Chao Phraya stretches and curves in front of me. Beyond the water I might find my endpoint.

I recall another line in Wright's letter to Nkrumah, "There will be no way to avoid a degree of suffering, of trial, of tribulation; suffering comes to all people, but you have within your power the means to make this suffering of your people meaningful, to redeem whatever stresses and strains may come."[8]

I consider texting these words to you. I think you'd appreciate them. But in place of a quick text I write this note to wish you well, to let you know this distance has helped me see you more clearly, and to apologize for not knowing when I will stand with you again on the same continent—because I am chasing opportunities you afforded me, pursuing a chance to do more than just survive.

Briny winds roll off the waves as the boat slogs against the river's forceful current. I check my watch. The immigration bureau offices may close before I reach them. Once I've crossed over this deep expanse, I don't know how long I'll wander or how far I'll stray. But I promise you, I will do my best to make the journey meaningful.

Love,

EDEM

---

8 Kwame Nkrumah, *Dark Days in Ghana* (New York: International, 1968).

ACKNOWLEDGMENTS

"Rays," *North American Review*; "Closing Procedures at Spencer Gifts," *Pithead Chapel*; "Till Next Time, Take Care of Yourselves and Each Other," *Vol. 1 Brooklyn*; "The Animals We Invent," *Awst Press*; "Cartography," *Numéro Cinq*; "Dogs in the Kingdom," *Slag Glass City*; "Figures," *The Nervous Breakdown;* "I'll Fly Away: Notes on Economy Class Citizenship," *The Rumpus*.

Many thanks to the friends and editors who saw earlier versions of these pieces:

Kali VanBaale, Sophfronia Scott, Panasit C., Douglas Glover, Kim Groninga, Chelsey Clammer, Tobias Carroll, Rigoberto González, Barrie Jean Borich, Mary-Kim Arnold, Liz Blood, P.E. Garcia, LK James, Emily Roberts, Tatiana Ryckman, and Wendy M. Walker.

I'm very grateful for the continued support from Tim Antonides, Jason Arment, Gayle Baldwin, Mike Blair, Ian Bodkin, Conleth Buckley, Catherine Buni, Mathieu Cailler, Colin Cheney & Anna Brown, Jennifer Cohen, Lydia Cole, Trinie Dalton, Jesse Dávila, Celeste Doaks, Madeleine Dubus, Courtney Ford, Arlia Frink, Christina Gustin, Jane Poirier Hart, Nick Hilbourn, Greg Hill, Mandy Holland, Justin Johnson, Susan King, Karen Kelly, Jacqueline Kharouf, Rhoda Knight, Anu Kumar, Jennifer Friedman Lang, Sunisa Manning, Josh Michael, Aisha Moorer, Damien Miles-Paulson, Mel Pennington, Amanda Cal Louise Phoenix, John Proctor, Richard Puffer, Victorio Reyes, Mary Rickert, Stephanie Rizzo, Elizabeth Schmul, Javier Starks, John Taylor Stout, Cheryl Telligman, Cedric Tillman, Lee Thomas, Rachel Thompson, Erin Record, Laura Reed, Ian Wallace, Michael Waskom, Cheryl Wright-Watkins, Graham Wood, Ben Woodard, and Natalie M. Zeigler.

With much love to my family: Dorothy Quist, Hammond J. Quist Jr., Dr. Faustina Quist, Sena Quist, Selorm Quist, Edward Ruffin, Charlie Van Ngo, and Pitchsinee Jiratra-Anant.

ABOUT THE AUTHOR

Donald Edem Quist is a writer and editor living in Bangkok, Thailand. He is author of the short story collection *Let Me Make You a Sandwich*. His work has appeared in *North American Review, The Rumpus, Hunger Mountain, J Journal, Queen Mob's Teahouse, Cleaver Magazine, Vol. 1 Brooklyn, Knee-Jerk Magazine, The Adroit Journal, Pithead Chapel, Numéro Cinq, Slag Glass City, Publishers Weekly*, and other print and online publications. He earned his MFA in Writing from Vermont College of Fine Arts.

Find him online at iamdonaldquist.com

"At a time when honest discussions of race, class, and violence are both necessary and too often simplistic, along comes Donald Quist. Perhaps this is what it takes—a uniquely positioned literary talent—to get us past familiar, easy categories. In *Harbors*, Quist assembles fragments, memories, conversations both real and imagined to reveal people in all their complexity and contradictions as well as the shifting lines of privilege and oppression. As Quist writes of three continents, his slim volume becomes my passport."

—Diane Lefer
author of *The Fiery Alphabet*

"In *Harbors*, Donald Quist gathers those moments of clarity that shape one man's consciousness about the black experience in a global environment. Whether it's growing up in the American South or seeking adventure in places as far away as Thailand, there's no escaping the fixed perceptions about class, race, and masculinity. Quist's poignant essays show us, however, what it's like to move through tension, conflict, and microaggression with hard-won dignity and grace—not unscathed, not unfazed, though certainly undefeated. A timely, stellar collection!"

—Rigoberto González
author of *Butterfly Boy: Memories of a Chicano Mariposa*

"In *Harbors*, Donald Quist bravely chronicles his attempts to find safe haven, to carve a space for himself and his humanity in a world where his blackness marks him for second-class citizenship. Quist sifts through the wreckages of his self—of love, of family, of escape across continents—to show readers the scars he's earned and the pain that still radiates from them. This is a much needed work, the rare collection that enlivens and enlarges the humanity of the reader."

—Rion Amilcar Scott
author of *Insurrections: Stories*